Atkins Diet for Beginners

The Easy-To-Follow Guide to Understand Atkins Meal Plan, Low-Carb Recipes and The Power of Protein for Burn Fat, Boost Your Health and Living a Low-Sugar Lifestyle

© **Copyright 2019 - All rights reserved.**

The content contained within this book may not be reproduced, duplicated or transmitted without direct written permission from the author or the publisher.

Under no circumstances will any blame or legal responsibility be held against the publisher, or author, for any damages, reparation, or monetary loss due to the information contained within this book. Either directly or indirectly.

Legal Notice:

This book is copyright protected. This book is only for personal use. You cannot amend, distribute, sell, use, quote or paraphrase any part, or the content within this book, without the consent of the author or publisher.

Disclaimer Notice:

Please note the information contained within this document is for educational and entertainment purposes only. All effort has been executed to present accurate, up to date, and reliable, complete information. No warranties of any kind are declared or implied. Readers acknowledge that the author is not engaging in the rendering of legal, financial, medical or professional advice. The content within this book has been derived from various sources. Please consult a licensed professional before attempting any techniques outlined in this book.

By reading this document, the reader agrees that under no circumstances is the author responsible for any losses, direct or indirect, which are incurred as a result of the use of information contained within this document, including, but not limited to, — errors, omissions, or inaccuracies.

Table of Contents

Introduction 1

Chapter 1: The Atkins Diet 3
    Who Is Dr. Robert Atkins? 3
    What Is the Atkins Diet? 4
    The Phases of the Diet 6
        Phase 1: Induction 6
        Phase 2: OWL (Ongoing Weight Loss) 7
        Phase 3: Pre-Maintenance 7
        Phase 4: Lifetime Maintenance 8
    The Principles of the Diet 8
    Is the Atkins Diet Effective? 9

Chapter 2: Benefits of the Atkins Diet 11
    Physical and Mental Benefits 11
        Improved Heart Health 11
        Weight Loss 11
        Controlled Blood Sugar Levels 12
        Prevents Metabolic Syndrome 13
        Controlled Appetite 13
        Improves Brain Function 14
        Increased Physical Endurance 14
        Clear Skin 15
        Improves Nutrition 15
        Decreases Inflammation 16
        Improves Digestion 16
        Prevents Cancer 17
        Decreases Visceral Fat 17
        Improves Sleep 18
        Maintain Your Weight 19
    Points to Keep in Mind Before Starting the Diet 20
        Carb Crash Is Real 20

    Learn to Count Carbs 22
    Sticking to the Atkins Diet Is Time-Consuming................... 24
    This Diet Is a Lifestyle Change 25

Chapter 3: Myths and Facts *26*

Chapter 4: An Introduction to Carbohydrates *32*

What Are Carbs? **33**
    Sugar.. 33
    Starch 34
    Fiber 34

Why Do We Need Carbs? **35**
    Energy 35
    Disease Risk 35
    Calorie Intake 36

Frequently Asked Questions **36**
    Should I Cut out Carbohydrates? 36
    Are Carbohydrates More Filling Than Proteins? 38
    If I Eat Carbohydrates, Which Ones Should I Eat? 39
    Do Carbohydrates Make You Fat? 39
    Do Carbohydrates Play Any Role in Exercise? 40
    When Should You Eat Carbs? 40

Chapter 5: An Introduction to Proteins *41*

Power of Proteins **41**

How Much Protein Can You Eat? **42**

Drawbacks of Consuming Large Quantities of Protein **43**

A Case Study on High-Protein Diets **44**

Choose Your Protein Wisely **46**

Chapter 6: The Phases of the Atkins Diet *48*

Phase 1: Induction **48**
    Guidelines 49
    Frequently Asked Questions 50

Phase 2: Ongoing Weight Loss **58**

Guidelines 59
Frequently Asked Questions 60

Phase 3: Pre-Maintenance 65
Listen to Your Body 65
Fine-Tuning Your Carbs 66
Frequently Asked Questions 67

Phase 4: Maintenance 68
Keeping Your Atkins Edge 68
Low-Carb Diet for Life 69
Frequently Asked Questions 69

Chapter 7: Atkins Diet Food List 71

Foods You Can Eat 72
Foundational Vegetables 72
Shellfish and Fish 72
Poultry 73
Meat 73
Eggs, Cheese, and Cream 74
Fats and Oils 74

Foods You Cannot Eat or Should Only Eat Sparingly ... 74
Grains and Grain Products 74
Fruits and Fruit Juice 75
Beans and Legumes 75
Alcoholic Beverages 75
Sugary Beverages 76
Nuts and Seeds 76
Sauces, Salad Dressings, and Condiments 76
Junk Foods and Sweets 77

Recommended Timing 77

Resources and Tips 79

Adjusting to Ketosis 79

Modifications 81

Chapter 8: How to Ease into the Atkins Diet 83

Set Goals 83

Determine the Right Atkins Plan for You 84
Only Keep the Approved Foods at Home 84
Plan Your Meals Using the Atkins Recipes 85
Stay Hydrated 85
Never Avoid Fats 86
Snack Frequently 86
Surround Yourself with Motivation and Support 87

Chapter 9: Atkins Recipes — Phase 1 (Induction) .. 88

Chocolate Slush 88
Shakshuka 89
Peppermint Hot Chocolate 91
Cajun Tofu 92
Beef Huevos Rancheros Over Canadian Bacon 93
Omelet-Stuffed Peppers 95
Scrambled Eggs with Herbs 96
Low-Carb Breakfast Muffins 97
Almond Pancakes 98
Sausage and Cauliflower Bake 99
Sheet Pan Brussels Sprouts and Egg and Bacon Hash 101
Low-Carb Sausage Breakfast 102
Buffalo Chicken Wings 104
Crustless Pumpkin and Ham Quiche 106
Low-Carb Mushroom Omelet 107
Red Cabbage Slaw with Mustard Vinaigrette 109
Beef and Broccoli Stir Fry 110

    Asian Steak Salad 112

    Beef Bolognese with Parmesan 114

    Baked Salmon with Bok Choy 116

    Balsamic Pork Loin with Roasted Rosemary Cauliflower 118

    Coconut Blondies 120

Chapter 10: Atkins Recipes — Phase 2 (Ongoing Weight Loss/Balancing) 122

    Easy Pizza Eggs 122

    California Breakfast Burrito 123

    Blackberry Smoothie 125

    Low-Carb Strawberry Popsicles 126

    Eggplant and Ricotta Rolls 127

    Easy Almond Butter Cookies 128

    Almond and Coconut Flour Muffins 129

    Stuffed Bell Peppers 131

    Chewy Cookies 133

    Citrus-Chili Shrimp 134

    Asparagus, Mushrooms, and Peas 136

    Low-Carb Donuts 137

Chapter 11: Atkins Recipes — Phase 3 (Pre-Maintenance) 140

    Atkins Low-Carb Wheat Bread 140

    Chicken Eggplant Casserole 141

    Bacon and Goat Cheese Salad 143

    Japanese Vegetable Tofu Soup 146

- Baked Quesadillas 147
- Beef and Spinach Soup 149
- Beef and Vegetable Stew 151
- Calabacitas 153
- Yogurt Berry Cups 154
- Yorkshire Pudding 155
- Pineapple-Coconut Granita 156
- Carrot Cake 157

Chapter 12: Atkins Recipes — Phase 4 (Maintenance) *159*
- Apple Oatmeal 159
- Breakfast Frittata 160
- Egg-Filled Bell Pepper Rings with Fruit 161
- Strawberry Mousse 162

Conclusion *164*
References *167*

Introduction

I want to thank you for choosing this book, and I hope you find it informative. The Atkins diet, created by cardiologist Dr. Robert Atkins, is, by far, one of the best diets developed in this century. The Atkins diet is one of the many low-carb diets that has been created over the last few decades. This diet will help you identify your carbohydrate tolerance and the right foods that you should consume to improve your metabolism. When Dr. Atkins was working on creating the diet, he put his patients on a diet that was low in sugar and carbohydrates. He based his entire experiment on the theory that every human being needed either fats or sugars to survive.

This book explains the Atkins diet and the different phases that you will go through when you are on it. You will learn about the different benefits that this diet has to offer, and more about the different foods that you can consume when you are on this diet. In addition, this book answers some questions about the different phases. You lose weight faster when you are on this diet since you do not consume too many carbohydrates or too much sugar. This book will also provide you with information about carbohydrates and protein, and why it is important to consume them.

Near the end, recipes have been provided that you can use when you begin the Atkins diet. These recipes will not take you more than thirty minutes to cook. However, you will need to put in some effort when you prepare your meals. There are times when you may find it difficult to either begin the diet or stick to the diet. This book sheds some light on how you can ease into the diet, and what you must do to stick with it.

Thank you for purchasing this book. I hope you find all the information you are looking for and love the recipes provided!

Chapter 1: The Atkins Diet

The Atkins diet, or the Atkins Nutritional Approach, is a diet that was created by an American cardiologist named Dr. Robert Atkins. He had first come across a diet in a journal which was published by the American Medical Association. He then identified another diet that he experimented with on himself. He found that the diet helped him lose weight. Only when he found that there were no repercussions to the diet did he start using it on his patients. However, before we move into the diet, let me give you a little insight into Dr. Robert Atkins.

Who Is Dr. Robert Atkins?

Dr. Robert Atkins pursued medicine at Cornell Medical College and received his degree in 1955. It was after Cornell that he decided to major in cardiology and complementary medicine. It was during his practice that he had tried to devise a diet that would ensure that his patients stayed healthy while they were losing weight. He had penned many books, the first of which was *Dr. Atkins' Diet Revolution.* He wrote many other books after the first, but he ensured that he never strayed away from his principles of what a diet had to be. He made sure that the diet that he created had a low intake of sugar and carbohydrates. Dr. Atkins passed away in 2003 after complications from brain surgery to remove a blood clot.

Now that you know about Dr. Atkins, let us move towards understanding what the Atkins diet is all about.

What Is the Atkins Diet?

The objective behind the Atkins diet is to ensure that you consume food that is low in carbohydrates. This was the first time that the world had been exposed to the benefits of a low-carbohydrate diet. There are four phases to this diet that include supplements for vitamins and minerals. However, there is a catch to this diet, too – you have to combine your diet with exercise. In his book, Dr. Atkins said that people tend to grow fat because they begin to ignore a few crucial facts that are critical to maintaining good health. He said that people had started to confuse good carbohydrates with refined carbohydrates.

While on the Atkins diet, you will find yourself losing weight since your body begins to burn the excess fat that it has been storing over the years, rather than burning the glucose that your body requires. This, in turn, provides you with immense energy. The shift between the burning of fat and the burning of glucose is called ketosis. When your body begins to lose out on glucose, it will lose out on insulin, too! This is when your body realizes that it must start the process of ketosis. At this point, your body will begin to empty the fat in the various reserves.

Your body tends to have lower amounts of insulin and glucose before you have consumed any food. Once you have eaten a good meal, you will find that the glucose in your body has increased. This automatically increases the levels of insulin in your body. When you consume too many carbohydrates, you will find that your body has too much glucose in the blood. Certain carbohydrates are considered good for your body and have a low or negligible impact on the glucose level in your blood. These are the carbohydrates that force your body into moving all the fat from the reserves into your body to provide you with a good amount of energy.

In his book, Dr. Atkins said that when people consume food that has a very low quantity of refined carbohydrates, they could trigger their metabolism, which would help burn more calories than any other diet. Your body begins to use all the energy reserves and rids your body of any extra calories. In the diet that he devised, Dr. Atkins focuses on a term called "net carbs." These net carbs are the difference between the carbohydrates that you have consumed and the fiber and sugar in your food. There has been enough research conducted that states that the alcohol in the sugars do not influence the levels of sugar in your blood. However, there are only a certain set of carbohydrates that you can eat – those with a lower glycemic constitution. He also stated that a person has to ensure that he or she consumes a lower quantity of saturated fats – preferably lower than 20% of his or her regular caloric intake.

According to Atkins, this diet would help reduce the amount of sugar that is found in the blood of a patient with type 2 diabetes. This change was also noted in patients who were not suffering from any metabolic conditions. The added benefit is that the person will never have to worry about medication if their blood sugar has regulated, though certain doctors disagree. Some have said that the diet does help to reduce blood sugar levels, but the patients will still need to undergo a dose of medication to ensure that they do not relapse.

The Phases of the Diet

The section above mentioned that there are four phases to the diet. Here, you'll get a general outline of these phases before we explore them in greater detail later in the book.

Phase 1: Induction

The first phase is where you begin by checking your caloric intake. You have to start cutting down on the number of calories that you are consuming. You must remember that your body will take some time to adapt to the changes that you make to your diet. When you find that your body has acclimated to the diet, you need to ensure that you determine the number of calories that you want to obtain through the carbohydrates that you consume. Limit the number of carbohydrates to 20 grams per day. It is always good to consume higher quantities of fruits and vegetables. You need to make certain that the vegetables and fruits you consume do not have a high constitution of starch.

Phase 2: OWL (Ongoing Weight Loss)

Once you have moved on from the induction phase, you need to work on trying to lose weight. You need to consume a balanced diet to ensure that you are obtaining the correct amounts of nutrients and fiber. Though these are obtained from carbohydrates, you will still need to consume a minimum of 25 grams to obtain these nutrients and fibers during the first week, and 30 grams during the second week. You will continue to consume 30 grams until you reach a point where you have stopped losing weight. When you find yourself at this plateau, you have to reduce your intake of carbohydrates by 5 grams every week until the day you find that you have begun to lose weight once again.

Phase 3: Pre-Maintenance

In the previous phase, you dropped your carbohydrate intake by 5 grams every week until you started to lose weight. You have to make sure that the loss of weight is gradual. In this phase, you need to increase the intake of carbohydrates by 5 grams every week until you find that you have begun to lose weight gradually.

Phase 4: Lifetime Maintenance

This is the phase where you will start introducing quite a few sources of carbohydrates. However, you have to ensure that you are maintaining your weight at all times. At this stage, you will find yourself in a state of well-being, which you have to ensure that you never let go of. You may find yourself gaining weight at some point during this phase. At this point, you will have to let go of a few of the new carbohydrates that you have begun to consume, and drop your intake of carbohydrates by 2 grams every week.

The Principles of the Diet

There are four underlying principles of the Atkins diet. You can use these principles to motivate yourself when you find yourself no longer losing any weight. You will begin to lose weight if you follow the diet strictly. The principles are:

1. You will find yourself losing weight.

2. Once you have lost the extra weight, you will find a way to manage the weight.

3. Since you have started consuming healthy food, you will be able to ensure that you are in great health.

4. You have created a strong foundation for yourself that will help you in preventing and overcoming any disease or disorder.

Is the Atkins Diet Effective?

You may have tried to follow many diets yet found yourself losing interest because you did not see any results. However, the truth is that, when you stick to any diet, you are bound to lose weight if you do not stray from the diet. This is true for the Atkins diet as well. A Stanford University team of researchers has conducted numerous studies and extensive research, and they concluded that a person following the Atkins diet has better blood pressure, lower levels of cholesterol, and a healthier weight loss when compared with other diets.

When you begin to follow the diet and abide by the principles of the diet, you can lose weight effectively and keep it off. It can be difficult to stick to the diet because it is hard for anybody to make immediate changes to their lifestyle. Dr. Atkins believed that it is only your lifestyle that will help you create a strong foundation towards living happily.

Though many people have tried this diet, it was found that only 10% of them continued to lose weight while the others plateaued and remained obese. While people all over the world are crazy about trying diets that will help them lose weight, not many have the diligence to stick to the plan they create for themselves. The truth is that diets with good carbohydrates or fewer bad carbohydrates work well, but people find it difficult to stick to the diet on account of getting bored of it or becoming frustrated from missing out on their usual foods. Multiple studies were conducted on a sample of people who followed the Atkins diet for three years. The results showed that a majority of the sample found it difficult to stick with the diet. Those who did were healthier than those who did not.

Chapter 2: Benefits of the Atkins Diet

Most doctors recommend the Atkins diet for people who are trying to lose weight quickly. However, when you consume a low-carb diet, you will benefit in many other ways as well. Numerous studies have been conducted to better understand how a low-carb diet helps to decrease weight and improve your health in other ways.

Physical and Mental Benefits

Improved Heart Health

Studies show that a low-carb and high-fat diet can help to reduce the risk of heart attack or stroke by up to 98%. People tend to develop heart disease when they consume a high-carb diet because their bodies produce and store excess insulin. Your heart health will improve when you reduce your carbohydrate intake. This diet raises the levels of good cholesterol in your body, and reduces the levels of bad cholesterol, blood pressure, and triglycerides.

Weight Loss

People who follow the Atkins diet and continue to eat healthily usually lose more than 100 pounds. That being said, you must remember that you will only lose weight if you adhere to the diet plan that you create for yourself. A low-carb diet will help to stimulate your body to burn the stored fat to produce energy. It is because of this reason that the Atkins diet will help you lose weight. You will, however, need to pay close attention to your intake of carbohydrates and count the number of carbohydrates you consume with each meal. You may be unable to stick to your weight loss plan and end up gaining back all of the weight that you lost if you do not keep track of the number of carbohydrates you are consuming. You will see fantastic results if you can add exercise to your plan as well.

Controlled Blood Sugar Levels

One of the major risk factors for both obesity and heart diseases is uncontrolled blood sugar levels. The first phase of the Atkins diet, the induction phase, will help your body process sugar more efficiently. Patients who take insulin before they embark on the Atkins diet can stop taking insulin shots soon since they changed their approach to nutrition. When you limit your carbohydrate intake, you will also be able to control the fluctuation in your blood sugar levels. Your sugar levels fluctuate when you consume foods that have more carbohydrates in them. One of the best ways to deal with blood sugar levels is to follow a low-carb and low-glycemic diet.

Prevents Metabolic Syndrome

Most risk factors and symptoms that lead to metabolic syndrome can be treated and cured through the Atkins diet. The Atkins diet is rich in nutrients, which will improve your body's function. Elevated cholesterol, hypertension, abdominal obesity, and diabetes are all addressed through the Atkins diet since you will increase your consumption of protein to help preserve your muscle mass. This muscle mass will ensure that your metabolism is functioning effectively and efficiently. This helps you burn all the necessary fat, thereby improving your health and well-being.

Controlled Appetite

The Atkins diet requires you to control your intake of carbohydrates, and it is for this reason that, while you are working on cutting down your intake of carbohydrates, you will have cravings for some foods that you used to eat. When you learn to eliminate the fluctuations in your blood sugar levels, you can control your appetite. The Atkins diet not only helps you eliminate any of your cravings, but it also keeps you satiated because you are consuming healthier meals. When you find yourself struggling with any cravings, you should try to break your meals down and include some snacks into your diet. You should also drink a lot more water and ensure that you do not crave food because of any emotional reasons. When you are more familiar with your body and mind, you can determine and identify what triggers your cravings, and you will learn to deal with those cravings properly.

Improves Brain Function

Some people believe that a low-carb diet has a negative effect on your brain functions. It is believed that your brain requires carbs to produce energy. When you follow the Atkins diet and you overcome the initial phase where you reduce your intake of carbohydrates, your body will adjust and shift to a new metabolic process. Since you will be consuming some brain-healthy fats and foods that are rich in vitamins, your body will produce more hormones, like serotonin, that will improve the function of the brain. You can also improve the survival and regeneration of brain cells, and the communication between the cells by consuming low-carb fruits like berries.

Increased Physical Endurance

Scientists know that the Atkins diet can help you reduce weight and improve your body's ability to efficiently and effectively burn fat. Studies are now being conducted to determine whether the diet can also help to improve the body's physical recovery and performance. According to some research, most athletes on the Atkins diet are very healthy, and they begin to achieve great things with extensive training and good genetics. When you restrict your intake of carbohydrates, you are rebooting your body's fat-burning program, which helps you reach significant levels of health and performance.

Clear Skin

Studies show that the Atkins diet helps curb or reduce some unpleasant and chronic skin conditions. The food that you consume on the Atkins diet can clear some of the itching, irritation, and redness caused by acne, vitiligo, eczema, and psoriasis. Even if you do not have any of these conditions, but are following the Atkins diet, you will find that your skin feels more radiant and is clear, healthy, and hydrated. Since your skin is healthier, you will also have healthier nails and hair. Your increased intake of nutrients will impact how you feel both on the inside and the outside.

Improves Nutrition

When you begin to focus on consuming unprocessed and whole foods, you will enjoy eating a greater quantity of nutrients like minerals, antioxidants, and vitamins. These will have a direct impact on your health and well-being. Foods that are rich in nutrients have a varied number of properties and provide a wide range of health benefits that you would not get if you were eating a pizza or a plate of spaghetti. You must ensure that your meals include the required proportion of fat and protein along with high fiber. This means that you should consume different kinds of foods that are rich in nutrients, thereby consuming a balanced diet.

Decreases Inflammation

Most people worry about inflammation, but what they forget is that this is a part of your body's defense mechanism. Any healthy individual will show signs of inflammation, especially during injury and illness. That being said, chronic inflammation can lead to some serious health issues like heart disease and cancer, and some neurological issues like Parkinson's or Alzheimer's. Most of this inflammation can be attributed to the spikes of insulin in the body. These spikes come from eating sugar, processed foods, and carbs. You can consume different types of food to reduce and prevent chronic inflammation, and most of these foods are recommended on the Atkins diet.

Improves Digestion

When you change your eating habits, it takes your body some time to adjust to these changes. That being said, it will be easier for your body to adjust to a low-carb diet since it is easier for your body to digest the food that you consume. Your digestive system will improve, and you will have reduced heartburn, bloating, and acid reflux. You may have issues with gas building up in your body when you initially start the Atkins diet, but when your body adjusts to your nutritional intake, you will find that you no longer have many issues with gas.

Prevents Cancer

The Atkins diet provides you with a nutritional plan that focuses on helping you get enough healthy fats. This will reduce the chances of you developing some types of cancer. When your body does not perform efficiently, there can be a growth of cancerous cells. This will create a breeding ground for any infection. One of the main reasons for this is uncontrolled blood sugar. The Atkins diet is known to maintain these levels. The reduced inflammation in the body will ensure that your body's immune system functions effectively. It will also help your body react well to stress.

Decreases Visceral Fat

Most people accumulate fat around their midsection, and this fat can lead to numerous health risks. This fat can impact most of the organs in your body since it produces more hormones and chemicals. Visceral fat can lead to numerous diseases, including colorectal cancer, cardiovascular diseases, and type 2 diabetes. It is difficult to lose visceral fat, yet it is extremely easy to put it on. It can be reduced if you exercise and sleep and eat well. The Atkins diet will help you tackle all three requirements, and it starts with your food intake.

Improves Sleep

Your body will no longer be under too much stress since you will increase the quantity of healthy fats and proteins in your diet. It is because of this that you can maintain your blood sugar levels. You will feel healthier and more energetic when you follow the Atkins diet. This will directly impact your sleep cycle, in the sense that you will be able to fall asleep much faster. Since you consume only healthy food on the Atkins diet, your brain will know when to keep you active and when to stay calm. This means that the quality of your rest will improve.

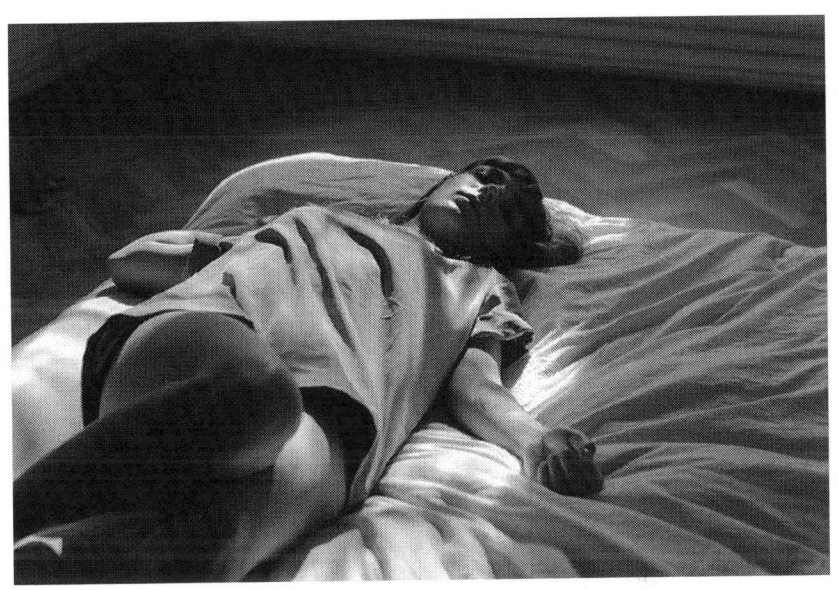

Maintain Your Weight

When you reach the final phase of the Atkins diet, you are in the maintenance mode. Most people will choose to return to their old eating patterns when they reach this phase, and they tend to gain back all the weight they have lost. Since the Atkins diet is more of a lifestyle than a short-term diet, it is considered to be a life-long nutritional approach. You will learn how to maintain your weight and improve your health. You only need to remember to introduce carbs slowly to your diet, but if you notice your cravings creeping in, you should reduce your intake immediately. The best way to maintain a healthy lifestyle while on the Atkins diet is to switch back and forth between the third and fourth phases of the diet. This will help you keep the extra pounds off.

Points to Keep in Mind Before Starting the Diet

Now that you have learned more about the Atkins diet and the benefits it has to offer, you may want to test the diet and see how it works for you. This section will shed some light on the points you should keep in mind when you do choose to follow this diet. There are some obstacles that you may come across when you follow this diet, especially when first starting out. The advantage is that you will feel so great while being on this diet that you will overlook these minor issues. You will find it easier to change your diet and lifestyle when you know what the benefits are. The Atkins diet is one of the best ways to maintain a healthy lifestyle.

Carb Crash Is Real

You may have been consuming too many carbohydrates before you started the Atkins diet. Because of this, you may feel slightly uncomfortable during your first few weeks into the diet because you will need to cut back on your food intake. You will find yourself missing some of your favorite foods and dealing with intense cravings. There are some ways in which you can distract yourself to help you move through this phase in the diet:

- Consume a lot of healthy fats and fiber. When you consume food that is rich in both of these nutrients, your body will be satiated. You can consume salads with lean protein or add flax seeds to your meal to obtain both fats and fiber.

- You should consume healthy snacks frequently. Make sure that you do not starve your body; consume a healthy snack every three hours. You should especially do this when you are suffering from any withdrawal symptoms. You can fight your cravings better if you can find different ways to avoid being hungry.

- Identify the different types of food you want to consume. You may not be allowed to consume most of your favorite foods, but there are still delicious foods that you can eat when you follow the Atkins diet. You should identify the healthy foods that you want to eat and that your body will crave instead of carbohydrates.

- You should always do something for yourself. You will be making great changes to your diet to help you improve your health and well-being. Therefore, you should try to do something you enjoy instead of giving in to an unhealthy craving. Take a bubble bath, meet up with your friends or family, or read a book.

There are some people who will still experience a carb crash even after they have overcome the withdrawal phase. These people have reported symptoms of feeling under the weather or just generally feeling "off." There are a few who will feel irritable, fatigued, or even shaky during this phase. These symptoms do disappear in a few days, but you can consume a serving of low-carb fruit to stop being overwhelmed by them.

Most of these symptoms are caused due to a decrease in salt consumption by the individual, since people will lose most of their water weight during the first few days. The quantity of sodium in your body will reduce for this reason. If you are unable to curb these symptoms by consuming a bowl of low-carb fruit, you should drink at least three cups of broth a day and ensure that you receive plenty of potassium.

Learn to Count Carbs

This may sound intimidating, but you will learn a lot about your body when you begin to count your intake of carbohydrates. The more you count your intake, the easier it will get for you. That being said, when you begin the Atkins diet, you will need to be very involved and aware when you go to the grocery store.

The first phase of the Atkins diet, the induction phase, has a very strict requirement that you should only consume up to 20 grams of carbohydrates every day. To keep on top of this, you will need to read the labels of every product that you pick up from the shelves and only add those foods that will help you stay within this limit. When you have passed this stage, you can add a few more low-carb foods to your diet, and you will eventually reach a point where you can start consuming more healthy carbs. You should only do this when you are certain that you will not gain weight. You must keep in mind that you will always need to think about the food that you are consuming.

When you read product labels, you must ensure that you check the serving size and count the number of carbohydrates in the food. If you want to consume a larger serving of some kind of food, you will need to triple the number of carbohydrates to ensure that you obtain the right estimate of what your intake may be.

Some people find it much easier to count their intake of carbohydrates by tracking their meals on an app. The app breaks the nutrients down, which helps you see how many carbohydrates you have consumed in one meal and over the course of the day. You can then begin to make some adjustments to ensure that you stay within the required range.

Sticking to the Atkins Diet Is Time-Consuming

If you are someone who often grabs some food on the go, you may need to make some huge changes to your lifestyle if you want to follow the Atkins diet. It is very difficult for people to find food that is readily available which still sticks to the rules of the Atkins diet. Therefore, you should be prepared to make meals for yourself or ask the chef to modify some food on the menu.

Grocery shopping will take more time than usual because you will need to learn more about the food you are consuming, and calculate your intake of the macros. You will get the hang of this soon enough. You will soon be able to walk into the grocery store and pick up the items that you can eat without thinking twice.

You will be spending a lot of time in the kitchen cooking for yourself and family, or even preparing for your meals in advance. If you have some extra time over the weekend, you should prepare in advance for the week. You can prepare all the food that you can eat when you are on the Atkins diet, and store the meals in the refrigerator. This is one of the best ways to teach yourself how to cook, and, much like counting carbs, this will also become second nature to you.

This Diet Is a Lifestyle Change

The Atkins diet is not only about losing weight; it is also about making some valuable changes to your lifestyle. These changes will help you achieve some long-term benefits. You will certainly lose inches around the waist and watch as your weight decreases, but if you want to maintain these results, you must look at the Atkins diet as more of a lifestyle commitment than just a diet.

If you want to stick to this diet, you must surround yourself with people who will support and motivate you. This support is the only thing that will guarantee that it becomes a life-long habit. It will certainly be difficult at first because you will need to stick to the Atkins-approved choices when you go out for drinks or dinner. That being said, if you are around people who want you to succeed, you can keep your social commitments when you are on the Atkins diet.

You should also try to pack some approved and healthy snacks for when people around you are snacking. People may bring chips or donuts to the office, or you may be invited to a party where there is a ton of junk food. You should make sure that you have some healthy snacks on you so you can prevent yourself from indulging in the food that you are not supposed to eat. When you do this, you will not be tempted to cheat on your new lifestyle.

Chapter 3: Myths and Facts

Regardless of whether you are new to the Atkins diet or have been following it for a while, you will come across some people who will tell you that a low-carb diet is very unhealthy to follow, especially for the long-term. They will give you numerous reasons why a low-carb diet is unrealistic to follow. Because of this, you should arm yourself with some facts. This chapter covers some of the myths surrounding low-carb diets like the Atkins diet.

Myth: You will consume a large quantity of saturated fats if you follow the Atkins diet, and saturated fats are the cause of many health issues.

Fact: Saturated fats are solid at room temperature, and are found in poultry, meat, palm and coconut oils, and dairy products. These fats are beneficial when they are consumed along with natural fats. When you restrict your intake of carbohydrates, your body will learn to burn more saturated fat instead of making it. Studies concluded that you lose a lot of weight during the first two phases of the Atkins diet. It is recommended that you do not consume too much saturated fat. You should ensure that you reduce your intake of carbohydrates. When it comes to the Atkins diet, you should only avoid consuming trans fats. If you consume too high of an amount of trans fat, you will increase the risk of developing heart diseases. It has also been shown that trans fats can lead to inflammation in the body. Trans fats are usually found in the foods that you are required to avoid eating, including baked goods, fried foods, crackers, cookies, snack foods, candy, vegetable shortening, and icings. If the food you are eating contains trans fats, you should ensure that the quantity is less than 0.5 grams. If you want to ensure that you do not consume any trans fats, you should read the nutrition label to make sure that there are no shortenings and that the oil used is not hydrogenated vegetable oil. If you do not want to consume any trans fats, you should avoid purchasing products that contain these ingredients.

Myth: Atkins is a high-protein diet and it will lead to kidney problems because of your protein intake.

Fact: You are going to consume enough protein when you are on the Atkins diet. You are required to consume anywhere between 12 and 18 ounces of protein each day. It is for this reason that the diet is not a high-protein diet. Most of the research around proteins does not necessarily provide the right information, and it is for this reason that one cannot say that it is bad to eat too much protein. For instance, the myth that proteins lead to kidney damage is not true. People who suffer from kidney issues are unable to clear the waste from their body. There is no evidence supporting the statement that people will develop kidney issues if they consume proteins, especially the quantity that you consume when you are on the Atkins diet. Studies have shown that people can lose weight when they consume more protein. You lose more weight because your hunger is satisfied and your body burns more calories. It is recommended that you consume at least 4 ounces of protein at every meal.

Myth: You cannot consume any vegetable when you follow the Atkins diet.

Fact: You are required to consume vegetables when you follow the Atkins diet, and will need to increase your servings in every phase of the diet. There are some vegetables that are the foundation of the Atkins diet. You may be wondering why you are being asked to eat vegetables when you need to reduce your intake of carbohydrates. Your body requires these carbohydrates to sustain and function efficiently. You need to remember that you are allowed to consume only some vegetables and not all of them. The Atkins diet is not like every other diet since it does not say that every vegetable is healthy. It provides a distinction. For example, you will learn that broccoli is better than potatoes since it helps you maintain your immunity. You will also learn that one serving of spinach is better than a bowl of peas. People tend to make the mistake of controlling their intake of vegetables because they want to reduce their intake of carbohydrates. You should never do this. All you need to do is limit your intake of starchy carbohydrates like potatoes, since these vegetables can hinder your weight loss or weight maintenance efforts. If you want to ensure that you do not consume too many carbohydrates but still consume vegetables, you should choose those vegetables that are rich in antioxidants and those that do not have too many carbohydrates.

During the first phase of the Atkins diet, you can consume 15 grams of carbs in the form of vegetables. You can consume 5 to 8 servings of vegetables depending on the vegetables that you choose to consume. You can consume 8 servings of salad greens and other raw vegetables like Swiss chard and kale, and cruciferous vegetables like Brussels sprouts and broccoli. You can also consume peppers, pumpkins, and tomatoes. Vegetables are an extremely important part of the Atkins diet. When you increase the number of carbs that you can consume and identify your tolerance to carbohydrates, you can either increase or decrease your intake of vegetables. From the second phase of the Atkins diet, you can consume berries, nuts, and some grains and fruit. So, you should try to enjoy different vegetables. You can tell people who advise you against the Atkins diet that you are choosing to follow a healthy eating program that will help you maintain your well-being and weight.

Myth: It is better to follow a low-fat diet instead of a low-carb diet like the Atkins diet.

Fact: Do not trust this statement too quickly. Studies show that a low-carb diet, like the keto diet or the Atkins diet, is always more effective when it comes to weight loss than a low-fat diet. Additionally, these studies also prove that a low-carb diet is safe and beneficial to people who are insulin resistant. Most people are resistant to insulin because they have an intolerance towards carbs. This is great news for people who are resistant towards insulin, since these people will need to identify a way to control their carb intolerance and insulin resistance. A controlled trial was conducted on a sample of thirteen people. This trial concluded that people who follow a low-carb diet can maintain the quantity of triglycerides and HDL cholesterol in their blood, and also control their blood pressure. This analysis supports previous studies that were conducted on the same subject. These studies did conclude that a low-carb diet is more effective when compared to a low-fat diet. If you have tested the Atkins diet, you will have observed many of the benefits that have been mentioned in the previous chapter.

Myth: You will not lose any fat on the Atkins diet, only water weight.

Fact: When you follow the Atkins diet, you will primarily lose water during the first few weeks. This is the case for any diet or exercise plan that you choose to follow. When you follow a low-carb diet and consume the right amount of protein and fat, you will shift your body into a metabolic state called ketosis. It is in this phase that the body will burn the stored fat to produce energy. This will result in weight loss. It is also important to remember that you will not be losing body mass; you will only be losing fat. Numerous studies have shown that it is easier to lose weight when you count your intake of carbohydrates instead of calories.

Chapter 4: An Introduction to Carbohydrates

There is a lot of debate around whether carbohydrates are good for the body or not, especially in the world of weight loss because of the introduction of different diets like the Ketogenic, Dukan, South Beach, and Atkins diets. The idea that carbohydrates are bad for people has left the world confused since there are numerous benefits to consuming carbohydrates. They are extremely important to maintain the health of the body and to maintain a healthy weight. Most experts believe that people need to understand that every carbohydrate is not the same. The quality, the type, and the quantity of carbohydrates in your diet are what will make a difference to you. It is important to reduce the quantity of free sugar from one's diet. Therefore, people should focus more on consuming healthy carbs and those carbs that provide fiber. Fiber is extremely good for your health, and numerous studies prove the same. This chapter provides all the information you will need to know about carbohydrates. You will also learn more about the benefits of consuming carbs, healthy sources of carbs, and how you should monitor your intake if you want to maintain a healthy weight.

What Are Carbs?

There are three macronutrients, or macros, that you must consume as a part of your diet, and carbohydrates are one of them. The other two macros are protein and fat. You should never expect any food to have only one of these macronutrients since most foods are a combination of fats, proteins, and carbohydrates. However, the proportion of the macros found in these foods will vary.

Sugar

Most adults and children consume a form of sugar called free sugars. These sugars are added to biscuits, chocolate, breakfast cereals, fizzy drinks, flavored yogurt, and other foods and drinks. You can even add these sugars at home when you cook. These sugars are also found in the food that you consume in restaurants. The sugar in maple, golden, and agave syrups, blossom nectars, unsweetened fruit juices, smoothies, vegetable juices, and honey is also considered free sugar. The sugar that is found naturally in fruit, vegetables, and milk is not considered free sugar.

Starch

Most food that comes from plants contains a large amount of starch. Food like rice, bread, pasta, and potatoes also contain a lot of starch, and these foods slowly release energy for your body throughout the day.

Fiber

There is a diverse range of compounds that you can find in the cell walls of the food that you obtain from plants. These compounds are known as fiber. The best sources of fiber are whole grain bread, beans and lentils, whole-wheat pasta, and vegetables.

Why Do We Need Carbs?

There are a number of reasons why it is important to consume carbohydrates:

Energy

For most people, carbohydrates are a main source of energy. If you eat a balanced diet, you will provide your body with at least 4 kilocalories of energy for every gram of carbohydrates that you eat. The carbohydrates are broken down in your body into glucose, and this glucose is absorbed by the bloodstream. Once the sugar is in the bloodstream, it will enter the cells in your body by using the insulin produced by the body. Your body will use glucose to produce energy, and this energy will be used when you perform any activity, including breathing. If your body does not use any glucose, it will be stored in your muscles and liver in the form of glycogen. If you consume too many carbohydrates, the excess glucose is stored as fat in your body. This fat will be used to produce energy in the long run. Carbohydrates that are rich in starch will release more sugar into your body.

Disease Risk

Vegetables, legumes, whole grains, whole wheat, and fruits are all very good sources of fiber. This compound is an important part of a balanced and healthy diet. Fiber will reduce the risk of constipation, reduce cholesterol levels in the body and also improve bowel health. There are numerous studies and research that show that foods rich in fiber are associated with a lower risk of bowel cancer, cardiovascular diseases, and type 2 diabetes. Most people do not consume enough fiber. The average person only consumes around 19 grams of fiber when they should ideally consume 30 grams of fiber a day.

Calorie Intake

Most carbohydrates contain fewer calories when compared to fats. Starchy foods are rich in fiber, and they also help to maintain your weight. When you replace sugary, fatty foods and drinks with food that is rich in fiber, you can reduce your caloric intake, thereby improving your chances of losing weight. You can keep your hunger satiated by consuming foods that are rich in fiber. You will still have to watch your portion sizes because you should always avoid overeating. It is also important to watch your fat intake when you cook your meals. Your caloric intake will increase if you consume too much fat in your meals.

Frequently Asked Questions

Should I Cut out Carbohydrates?

It is easy for people to survive without consuming any sugar, but it would be hard to expect people to remove carbohydrates from their diets since carbohydrates are the main source of energy for your body. That being said, if you do want to reduce your weight, it is best to limit your intake of carbohydrates to ensure that your body will learn to burn the stored fat to produce energy. When you reduce your intake of carbohydrates, you will automatically reduce the amount of fiber that you consume. As mentioned earlier, fiber is extremely important for your body.

If you do choose to limit your intake of carbohydrates, it is best to consume food that is rich in fiber, like legumes, vegetables, and fruits. These foods are also rich in nutrients like vitamin B, calcium, and iron. You must ensure that you do not reduce your carbohydrate intake by too much since it could lead to some health issues. You may develop some deficiencies when you cut carbohydrates out of your diet. To avoid developing such health issues, experts suggest that you consume some supplements.

When you replace carbohydrates, you will tend to eat more protein and fat, and this may increase your intake of trans fats. This will increase the cholesterol in your blood, which could lead to heart diseases. It is for this reason that you should only stick to consuming healthy fats to avoid developing any health issues. When you do not consume enough carbohydrates, your body will not have sufficient glucose. Your body will then shift into the metabolic state called ketosis where it will burn the stored fat to produce energy. Ketosis can cause weakness, nausea, dizziness, irritability, and dehydration in the beginning. However, once your body adapts to this metabolic state, you will lose weight and also experience the benefits of ketosis.

It is important to remember to limit your intake of food that is rich in sugar. You should try to include healthy sources of carbohydrates in your diet, like vegetables, fruits, low-fat dairy products, legumes, whole grains, and potatoes.

Are Carbohydrates More Filling Than Proteins?

Both carbohydrates and proteins provide the same number of calories per gram. Factors like the variety, the quantity, and the type of food you are eating will influence your sensation of feeling full. There are external behavioral and environmental factors, like availability of food choices and portion sizes, that will also affect your appetite and hunger. It is important to understand that every individual is different from the other. Protein-rich foods like fish, seeds, nuts, beans, eggs, meat, and legumes are all a part of a balanced and healthy diet. You must ensure that you only consume a limited quantity of these foods. You must always have a higher amount of fruits and vegetables in your diet.

If I Eat Carbohydrates, Which Ones Should I Eat?

Most people tend to eat cakes, pastries, chocolates, and sweets, and drink soft drinks and other beverages that have too much sugar. They do not care about eating healthy carbohydrates or fiber. It is for this reason that these people are overweight and almost never lose weight. It is important that you eat foods like nuts, legumes, fruits, and vegetables to provide your body with the required carbohydrates and nutrition.

Do Carbohydrates Make You Fat?

You will gain weight if you consume a large amount of carbohydrates. When you consume too many carbohydrates, your body will break them down into sugar, which it will use to produce energy. When this happens, your body will never use the stored fat to produce energy. It is for this reason that people who consume more carbohydrates tend to put on more weight. That being said, when you compare 1 gram of carbohydrates with 1 gram of fat, the latter has more calories. If you want to lose weight, you should count both your caloric intake and carbohydrate intake, since foods that have a lot of sugar are rich in calories. When you increase your caloric intake, you will tend to put on more weight. There are numerous studies that prove that food rich in carbohydrates is directly associated with high energy, which can lead to weight gain.

Do Carbohydrates Play Any Role in Exercise?

All the macros, carbohydrates, proteins, and fats, provide sufficient energy, but when you exercise, your muscles only rely on carbohydrates for energy. You must top up glycogen stores in your muscles regularly if you want to maintain your levels of energy when you exercise. However, it is never a good idea to eat too many carbs, since this will increase the level of sugar in your blood. A low-carb diet may initially make you feel weak when you exercise, but once your body adapts to it, it will begin to provide your muscles with energy by burning the stored fat.

When Should You Eat Carbs?

There is no evidence to prove that one time is better than any other when it comes to eating carbohydrates. Most experts recommend that you should base your meals around some starchy food and also choose some high-fiber varieties of food whenever possible.

Chapter 5: An Introduction to Proteins

A low-carbohydrate and moderate-protein diet has been the hottest thing since people started losing weight by following these diets. Most bodybuilders and athletes are doing their best to consume a protein-rich diet to lose weight quickly and to increase their muscle mass.

Power of Proteins

Protein is an important macronutrient that every human being must consume, and it is an important component of every cell in the human body. Nails and hair are only made of protein, and your body uses protein to repair and build tissues. Your body also uses protein to make hormones, enzymes, and other necessary chemicals. Protein is an important building block of skin, blood, muscles, cartilage, and bones.

Protein is a macronutrient like fat and carbohydrates, and it is important for you to consume a large quantity of macronutrients. You only need small quantities of minerals and vitamins, which is why they are called micronutrients. Unlike carbohydrates and fats, your body does not store protein, and it is because of this that proteins do not add to your weight. You may think that you can constantly consume protein, but this is not the case. The truth is that you need very little protein, but this protein should come from good sources.

How Much Protein Can You Eat?

Some people believe that it is a good idea to eat extra protein if you want to build more muscle. While that may be true, the only way you can build muscle is through exercise. Your body only requires a moderate amount of protein to function. You do not get any extra strength when you consume extra protein. According to the Department of Health and Human Services:

- Active men and teenage boys should consume around 60 grams of protein each day. They should split this between three meals.

- Children between the ages of two and six, older people, and sedentary women should consume two servings of protein each day for a total of 35-40 grams.

- For active women, older children, sedentary men, and teen girls, it is recommended that you should consume two servings of protein a day for a total of 50 grams.

If you consume an 8-ounce steak, that will likely be all or most of the protein you need for the day, since the average 8-ounce steak contains 45-50 grams of protein. However, you are also consuming a lot of saturated fat with that steak, which can block your arteries.

Drawbacks of Consuming Large Quantities of Protein

People who consume large quantities of protein believe that they can pack all the extra protein in their body. Experts, however, want them to exercise caution. There is sufficient evidence that suggests that people who eat a high-protein diet will excrete calcium in their urine. This means that the body is releasing all the calcium that it has stored in the body. It is for this reason that you should only consume a moderate amount of protein.

There are also some obvious concerns about consuming a diet that is rich in protein. Some of the foods that people shun when they follow a low-carb diet include fruit and vegetables, and these foods are some of the best sources of fiber, antioxidants, and vitamins. These are the nutrients that help to prevent the development of disease. Animal foods are rich in protein, but are also high in saturated fats, which increases the risk of developing heart diseases, diabetes, and other types of cancer.

The American Heart Association states that, when people reduce their intake of carbohydrates, they tend to consume food that has large quantities of fat. This will increase their cholesterol levels and, as a result, increase the risk of developing cardiovascular diseases. The AHA also noted that people who cut out carbs entirely and only focus on consuming protein would consume too much salt and not enough magnesium, calcium, and potassium. These nutrients are found in vegetables, whole grains, and fruits.

A Case Study on High-Protein Diets

Many people are unaware of the effects of a long-term, high-protein diet. People believe that these diets can be safe and are effective. There are a few questions that you need to ask yourself before you choose to begin a high protein diet:

- Does your body burn more fat when you consume a high-protein diet?
- Does a high-protein diet keep you satiated for a longer period of time?
- When you consume a high-protein diet, do you reduce your caloric intake?
- Does a high-protein diet aid in weight loss?

For the most part, the answer to all the questions above is yes. The human body can convert protein into glucose and provide the body with energy. It will, however, take the body twice the amount of effort to convert protein into glucose when compared to converting carbohydrates or fats into glucose. The extra effort that your body puts in will use the calories that you consume.

When it comes to feeling satiated, studies show that high-protein diets decrease your appetite and help keep you feeling full for longer. A high-protein diet is better than a high-carbohydrate diet. In addition to this, people who consume a high-protein diet tend to consume fewer calories, and this automatically translates to weight loss.

Choose Your Protein Wisely

It is important for you to choose the protein you eat wisely if you want to improve your health and lose weight. It is not a good idea to consume processed meat like sausages, deli meats, and hot dogs since they increase the risk of developing type 2 diabetes, colorectal cancer, and cardiovascular diseases. You will find it difficult to maintain your weight if you consume these proteins regularly, which will damage your body.

Nutritionists and experts recommend that you obtain the required quantity of protein from the following foods:

- **Fish** - Fish has less fat when compared to other meat and is also rich in omega-3 fatty acids, which improve the heart's health.

- **Poultry** - If you remove the skin from the meat, you can reduce the amount of saturated fat that you will consume.

- **Beans** - Beans have more protein when compared to any other vegetable, and they are also rich in fiber. These can keep you full and satisfied for many hours.

- **Nuts** - You can gain 6 grams of protein by eating an ounce of almonds, and this is a good substitute to broiled ribeye steak.

- **Whole Grains** - One slice of whole wheat bread will give you fiber and at least 3 grams of protein.

If you are a vegetarian, you should consume legumes and soy since they can provide the same amount of protein as meat. You can consume nuts as a snack or breakfast since they are not only a source of protein, but also a source of healthy fat. When you decide to reduce your intake of carbohydrates, you can consume more protein. Remember to never lose sight of the big picture.

Chapter 6: The Phases of the Atkins Diet

Here, we will take an in-depth, detailed look at each phase of the Atkins diet before answering some of the frequently asked questions about each phase.

Phase 1: Induction

The first phase of the Atkins diet is the induction phase, and it is not easy for everyone to complete this phase. If you do not have too much weight to lose, or you are already a vegetarian, you should begin with the second phase of the Atkins diet. You should meet a nutritionist to help you calculate your BMI. Your BMI will help you decide which phase you should begin with.

You should start with Phase 1 if you fit any or all of the criteria listed below:

- You want to lose more than 14 lbs.
- You either have a slow metabolism or are inactive
- You have regained all the weight that you initially lost
- You want to lose some weight quickly

Guidelines

You must stick to some rules when you begin the induction phase of the Atkins diet.

- You should consume 3 meals every day. If you are often hungry, you can spread your meals out during the day and consume 4 or 5 smaller meals.

- You should ensure that your body is not in the fasting state for longer than 6 hours a day.

- You should consume at least 120 grams of protein-rich food in every meal that you eat.

- Ensure that your intake of carbohydrates is only 20 grams.

- A majority of your carbohydrate intake should come from salads or cooked vegetables.

- Ensure that you receive all the nutrients you need by consuming a few multivitamin or multimineral tablets. You can also consume an omega-3 fatty acid supplement.

- Drink at least 8 glasses of water every day. You can also swap the glasses of water with other acceptable drinks.

The induction phase will help you distinguish between your need to eat and your actual hunger. You can do this by changing the food that you consume to ensure that you stick to the rules of the Atkins diet. Your appetite will slowly begin to decrease, so you must consume nutrient-rich food to ensure that you obtain the required nutrients.

When you are hungry, make sure that you eat the required quantity of the food and do not overeat. If you are not sure if you are hungry or if you are simply bored, you should drink a glass of water and wait for 10 minutes. You can then decide if you are still hungry. Do not consume a huge meal and do not skip your meals. You can eat a low-carb snack instead.

Frequently Asked Questions

Can I Consume Seeds and Nuts During the Induction Phase, Especially When They Have Carbohydrates?

The Atkins diet is about controlling your intake of carbohydrates and consuming those foods that are nutrient dense. You can consume different seeds and nuts, depending on your body fat percentage. You should also look at the different percentage of protein and carbohydrates in the nuts and seeds that you want to consume. You should only consume these foods after the first two weeks of the induction phase, and you can start consuming some nuts and seeds if you are losing weight steadily during the first phase. Remember to avoid consuming any nuts and seeds that have molded since that could trigger an allergic reaction.

It is more difficult to consume nuts and seeds in moderation since you often find them for sale in large quantities and you might end up eating more than just a few. They are addictive. You should try to buy a small packet of nuts or seeds, so you do not indulge or overeat.

How Many Calories Am I Allowed to Consume During the Induction Phase?

When you follow the Atkins diet, you will need to count the carbohydrates that you consume, but not the calories. You are allowed to consume only 20 grams of carbohydrates per day during the induction phase. When you move to the next phase of the Atkins diet, you can gradually increase your daily carbohydrate intake in 5-gram increments. You must ensure that you count your carbohydrates. For the purpose of weight loss, it is suggested that you stick to the required number of calories. The average male should consume around 2,000 calories a day while the average female should consume at least 1,800 calories a day. You should ensure that you stick to the list of foods that you are allowed to consume during the induction phase.

Studies show that you can burn more calories when you are on a controlled carbohydrate diet program as opposed to a high-carbohydrate and low-fat diet. As mentioned earlier, you can improve your metabolism when you control your carbohydrate intake. This does not mean that you can gorge yourself, binge, or consume too much food.

The goal of the Atkins diet is to ensure that you learn new eating habits that will enable you to maintain a healthy lifestyle and weight. This means that you will need to change your old habits, such as controlling the size of your portions. You must also avoid overeating.

I Am Not Too Far from My Ideal Weight, so Would It Be Okay If I Did Come off the Atkins Diet and Continue to Eat Healthily?

It is great that you have almost reached your ideal weight. If you are very close to your ideal weight, you should ensure that you move to the second phase and not give up on the Atkins diet.

You should avoid switching back to your older eating habits and prevent consuming too many carbohydrates immediately since it will lead to water retention and weight gain. It is a good idea to reintroduce your intake of carbohydrates since it will help you lose weight. You will also be able to test your tolerance. Follow all the steps of the Atkins diet until you find the right carbohydrate balance for your body. You can only consume healthy food if you want to maintain your ideal weight.

You can move slowly into Phase 2, especially if you are close to reaching your ideal weight. You can slowly add more carbohydrates into the diet by introducing 5 more grams every day. This means that you can begin to consume nuts, seeds, and berries, as well as some dairy products. You can also begin to consume some Atkins bars if necessary. You should only start adding more carbohydrates to your diet if you are 10 lbs. away or less from your ideal weight.

I Was Losing Weight, but Have Stopped Losing It. What Should I Do Now?

If you have not started counting your daily consumption of carbohydrates, you must start now. There are studies that show that people will continue to stick to their weight loss plan only when they track their consumption of carbohydrates. You must ensure that you consume at least 15 grams of your daily carbohydrates through boiled vegetables. You must remember to be patient, and remember that your weight loss will begin to slow, especially when you are nearing your ideal weight. If you stick to the meal plan, your body will slowly begin to lose weight.

Is It Okay for Me to Consume Yogurt During the Induction Phase? If Yes, What Kinds of Yogurt Can I Consume?

You are not allowed to consume yogurt during the induction phase since it contains too many carbohydrates. You can reintroduce yogurt to your diet during the next phase of the Atkins diet. Since yogurt is on rung 5 of the ladders, you can only introduce these carbohydrates after you have reintroduced seeds, nuts, cherries, and berries.

You must remember to consume whole milk and unsweetened yogurt instead of the low-fat versions of yogurt. The latter version of yogurt is high in sugar and has more carbohydrates. It is ideal to consume plain Greek yogurt since it is low in carbohydrates, and you can add some flavor to the yogurt by mixing in some nuts and berries. You must make sure to check the label on the yogurt container for the amount of sugar in the yogurt. You should only consume natural yogurt since that will only contain around 5 grams of carbohydrates per serving.

Can I Consume Sausages During This Phase?

There are some sausages that contain carbs and other fillers, so you must check the nutrition label before you consume them. Some brands that make organic, low-carb sausages are Applegate Farms and Jones Dairy Farm. You can purchase these from any supermarket.

I Want to Follow a Vegetarian Atkins Diet. Is It Okay for Me to Consume Quorn Products Instead of Meat?

A vegetarian can follow the Atkins diet by substituting meat with Quorn products. You can also increase your intake of protein by consuming cheese, eggs, and tofu. Make sure that you also consume olives, oils, fats, and avocado since they provide your body with the required fiber, healthy fats, and nutrients that your body requires. There are numerous recipes that you can use when you are on the Atkins diet, and this book, in later chapters, covers some of the most delicious recipes. Before you add Quorn products to your diet, read the nutrition label to calculate your intake of carbohydrates. You must remember to consume a small number of carbohydrates, and also include the other macronutrients. For example, if you consume Quorn burgers, you will consume 4 grams of carbohydrates per burger. So, it is important that you consume the required amount of protein and avoid consuming excess amounts of carbohydrates.

You can choose to begin with the second phase of the Atkins diet where you are allowed to consume 30 grams of carbohydrates per day. This means that you can start with consuming berries, nuts, and seeds. If you only need to lose 4 lbs., you can start with the third phase and choose the right foods that will help you lose weight slowly. You can add extra flaxseed oil, rapeseed oil, or olive oil to vegetables and salads. This will help to compensate for the low amount of fat that you consume. It is also recommended that you consume some supplements that will boost your overall health.

I Am Often Constipated When I Follow the Atkins Diet. How Can I Avoid This?

It is common to experience some constipation during the first few weeks of the induction phase since there is a slight change in your diet after reducing your consumption of fruits and vegetables. This will reduce your fiber intake. Consume at least 15 grams of carbohydrates per day from vegetables alone, and avoid consuming other carbohydrate-rich food. Your body will soon adjust to this new phase and constipation will no longer be a problem. When you choose to add more carbohydrates to your diet, make sure that you only obtain these carbohydrates through vegetables and fruit. You can try different remedies if you still suffer from constipation. Consume a sufficient amount of water and remain hydrated as well. Alternatively, you can consume some fiber that you obtain from ground flaxseed, wheat bran, and psyllium husks.

Why Can't I Consume Alcohol During the Induction Phase of the Atkins Diet?

It is important that you do not drink any alcohol during the induction phase of the Atkins diet. That being said, you can drink a little more alcohol during the next few phases of the Atkins diet. If you drink alcohol, your body will burn that to produce energy and not the fat in your body. Alcohol will never act in the same way that healthy carbohydrates do, and it is for this reason that it does not interfere with the burning of stored fat in the same way that carbohydrates and sugars do.

When Can I Progress from the First Phase to the Second?

You can move from the first phase of the Atkins diet and slowly add more carbohydrates to your diet when you have lost most of the weight that you want to lose in the first phase. Alternatively, you can move to the second phase of the Atkins diet when you are bored or frustrated with the different foods that you are allowed to consume in the induction phase. You can consume a wider variety of foods during the next phase of the Atkins diet.

Phase 2: Ongoing Weight Loss

If you do not have to lose too much weight, you can directly start with Phase 2. You can always speak to nutritionists to learn more about which phase you should start off with by calculating your BMI. You can begin with the second phase of the Atkins diet if you fit any of the criteria mentioned below:

- You want to lose less than 14 lbs.

- You do not feel the need to rush to lose weight quickly

- You want to enjoy a variety of foods but also want to lose weight

- You are a vegetarian

Guidelines

In this phase, you can slowly increase your intake of carbohydrates. This will help you improve your tolerance towards carbohydrates. You can add different Atkins food products to your diet, including berries, seeds, nuts, and some cheeses.

- When you increase your intake of carbohydrates gradually, you will note the number of carbohydrates that you can consume while also working towards reaching your ideal weight. This will help you create the foundation for your low-carb diet and lifestyle.

- You must remember to be patient since you will lose weight slower during this phase when compared to the first phase. You should stick to the rules of the phase since this will help you reach your goal.

- If you are a vegetarian, you can start by consuming at least 30 grams of carbohydrates daily.

- If you want to identify your tolerance to carbohydrates, you can add an extra 5 grams of carbohydrates every week.

- You are allowed to include nuts, berries, seeds, and specific cheeses to your diet.

- You can also include different Atkins products to your diet.

- You should monitor your intake of carbohydrates, and you can do this through different carb counter applications.

- Consume a lot of natural fats.

- You should continue to consume multimineral, omega-3, and multivitamin supplements.

- You should consume at least 8 glasses of water, or comparable substitute, per day.

Frequently Asked Questions

If I Only Consume Twenty Grams of Carbohydrates a Day, Can I Consume a Slice of Whole Wheat Bread or Grain Bread, Which Only Contains 20 Grams of Carbs?

There are two reasons why most nutritionists will advise you against following this approach. The first is that all carbohydrates cannot be considered equal. The Atkins diet is a nutritional approach that was designed to prevent spiking of blood sugar. This will help to prevent the overproduction of insulin in the body. When you move from the first phase of the Atkins diet, you can add a few more vegetables to your diet, followed by nuts and seeds. You can also add some berries to the diet followed by grains and legumes if you are still losing weight. Bread that is made from 100% whole-wheat flour will still contain refined carbs that will make your body start storing fat since your body will begin to produce more insulin. If you are still losing weight, you can increase your intake of carbohydrates, and can occasionally consume whole grain bread.

Secondly, the Atkins diet is not only about losing weight rapidly; it is also about learning how to eat different types of carbohydrates and maintain a healthy lifestyle for the rest of your life. There are some foods that are packed with antioxidant vitamins and healthy phytochemicals. When you have reached your ideal weight and have struck a balance between the carbohydrates and other macros, you can begin to consume other types of food.

Is It Okay for Me to Start Drinking Alcohol Now That I Am in the Second Phase of the Atkins Diet?

Your body will burn the alcohol to provide it with energy when that is available. So, when there is alcohol in your body, it will not burn the stored fat to provide energy. This will not stop the weight loss journey, but will postpone it. Alcohol does not get stored in the body in the form of glycogen, but will switch your body back into the fat burning mode, called lipolysis, once the alcohol has been used up fully. You must keep in mind that your consumption of alcohol will increase the yeast-related symptom that will interfere with this weight loss journey. It is okay to consume the occasional glass of wine if you are certain that it does not slow down your weight loss. You will only need to remember to count your intake of carbohydrates. It is okay to consume gin, vodka, and scotch, but you must ensure that you do not mix these spirits with tonic water, non-diet soda, or juice since these all contain a lot of sugar. Diet mixers and diet tonics are allowed during this phase. If you notice that you stop losing weight when you start consuming alcohol, you should stop consuming it immediately.

I Lost Weight When I Was on the First Phase Of The Diet, and During the First Few Months of the Second Phase of the Diet. The Scale No Longer Budges. How

Do I Change This?

Before you assume that you have a problem, you should ask yourself a few questions:

1. Do your clothes fit you better?
2. Are you feeling better now than you did before?
3. Are you losing inches and not pounds?
4. Do you see yourself losing weight, but at a very slow rate?

You will need to continue the diet for a longer time, but you can make some modifications to the diet. These modifications include:

- Decreasing your intake of carbohydrates by 5 or 10 grams
- Decreasing your intake of protein and increasing the amount of fat to the diet
- Finding and eliminating the hidden carbs in processed foods and lemon juice since they may contain some sugar
- Increasing your level of activity
- Drinking at least 8 glasses of water every day

- Reducing your intake of artificial sweeteners, excess protein, and cheese

What Is Carb Creep and How Can I Avoid It?

When you begin to add more carbohydrates to your diet after moving from the first phase of the diet to the second phase of the diet, you may tend to stop counting your intake of carbohydrates. You will regain all the weight that you have lost during the first phase of the diet if you stop this. It is for this reason that it is important that you increase your intake of carbohydrates gradually. You can increase your intake by 5 grams every week, and only introduce one new type of food to the diet at a time. That way, you can immediately notice if there is some food that is increasing your cravings, which leads to overeating. Another way that you can control your intake of different types of food is to maintain a food diary, which will help you spot your binging or cravings. For instance, if you see that you are hungry a few hours after eating nuts, you should remove nuts from your diet and substitute it with something else. You can then see if your hunger disappears.

When Can I Move from Phase 2 to Phase 3?

When you are close to nearing your ideal weight, which means you are only 5 or 10 pounds from your target weight, you should move to the next phase of the diet. You can increase the variety of food that you can consume. You will also need to learn more about the different kinds of food you can consume without gaining weight. You should increase your intake of carbohydrates by 10 grams every week. As long as you continue to lose weight slowly but at an imperceptible rate, you can add whole grains, like whole wheat bread or brown rice, and starchy vegetables to your diet. If you realize that these foods are increasing your cravings or are making you gain weight, you should stop eating those foods immediately.

Phase 3: Pre-Maintenance

When you are nearing your ideal weight, you must remember that it is always a good idea to lose that weight slowly. This phase is more about building your tolerance towards carbohydrates, so you should know what works for you and what does not before you move to the next phase of the Atkins diet. You must remember that we are all very different, so what may work for you does not necessarily work for another person. If you are struggling to stick to the diet or have a lot of questions, you can speak to some professionals or any other member in the Atkins community for some extra support.

Listen to Your Body

During the third phase of the Atkins diet, you can increase

your carb intake by at least 10 grams every week. This will help you find your carbohydrate balance, and the ideal level will help you reach your ideal weight. It will also ensure that your weight stays at the ideal weight. You must remember that your body is different from another person's body, so it is only because of trial and error. You should take this at your own pace and always pay attention to your body.

When you reach your ideal goal and are able to keep it at that weight for over a month, you will know what types of carbs you are allowed to eat. You will also know the amount of carbs that your body will be able to handle and what it cannot.

Fine-Tuning Your Carbs

If you realize that you stop losing weight or are craving more food, you should drop your intake of carbohydrates by at least 10 grams for a week. You can then introduce at least 5 grams of carbohydrates to find your tolerance and level. This is the final stage, where you will be fine-tuning your carbohydrate intake. You will learn to strike a balance between your ideal weight and your intake of carbohydrates.

You must remember that your weight loss will slow down when you work on striking the right balance. You should be patient and also stick to a few rules to ensure that you find the right limit, which will help you maintain the right weight.

- If you are trying to strike a balance between your intake of carbohydrates and your ideal weight, you should add 10 grams of carbs to your diet every week.

- During this phase, you are allowed to add more grains, fruits, and starchy vegetables to your diet.

- You should monitor your intake of carbohydrates.

- You can only consume 8 glasses of water every day.

Frequently Asked Questions

I Am Able to Follow the Atkins Diet and Am Now in the Third Phase of the Atkins Diet, but My Appetite Has Begun to Increase. Why Is This Happening and How Can I Manage It?

Your appetite can return when you no longer are in the fat burning mode. You may have added some food to your diet, which will make it hard for you to maintain your blood sugar levels. This will also make it hard for you to control your cravings and will contribute to increasing your appetite. You should examine the different types of food you have added to your diet, and also determine if this food contains refined grains or sugar. Maintain a regular intake of fat and protein. If you find it easier to control your hunger by consuming food that adheres to the rules of the Atkins diet, you should eat more of it. If everything fails, you should stop adding more foods to your diet and then control your appetite.

When Can I Move from the Third Phase to the Fourth Phase?

When you have learned to maintain your weight for at least 4 weeks, you will have moved to the fourth phase. In the fourth phase, you can begin to consume whole foods. On some occasions, you can indulge in eating some dessert or a slice of cake. That being said, you will need to continue to avoid products that contain white flour and sugar. It is only then that you can maintain your weight.

Phase 4: Maintenance

You have finally done it! You have reached your ideal weight, and have managed to stay there. This is wonderful, and it is something you truly need to be proud of. The fourth phase of the Atkins diet is about helping you maintain your weight and a low-carb diet in the future. You will be able to maintain your ideal weight when you follow this diet.

Keeping Your Atkins Edge

You are now aware of the ins and outs of the low-carb diet and are aware of what you can eat and what your body can take. You obviously will not be surprised to know that you cannot stop working on your weight simply because you have reached the ideal weight. You can maintain your weight indefinitely if you can maintain the carb balance for a few weeks or months. There may come a time when you may let things slip, and you will begin to gain weight because you have some cravings. Do not panic when that happens. You can always get back to your ideal weight by simply counting and controlling your intake of carbohydrates.

Low-Carb Diet for Life

When you are going forward, you can continue to eat the same foods that you previously enjoyed in the third phase. The only adjustment that you make is to reduce your intake of fats as your intake of carbs increases. When you are active, you can maintain the right balance and also lead to a healthy lifestyle. If you are not exercising already, you must get moving and regularly exercise. You can keep your weight off by simply reducing the risk of developing any illnesses.

Frequently Asked Questions

Once I Reach My Ideal Weight, What Food Can I Eat to Maintain My Weight?

When you are on the Atkins diet, you can consume some of the best foods you can every purchase. You will learn more about the different foods you can eat in the next chapter. You will need to identify your carbohydrate tolerance. This will help you learn more about your metabolism and activity level. Men and younger people will have higher metabolisms than women and older people. If you have a high-carbohydrate threshold and also exercise regularly, you can consume starchy vegetables, legumes, beans, fruits, and whole grains in moderation. If you have a low-carb threshold and are not very active, you will need to limit your intake of carbohydrates. In either case, you should still consume whole foods and avoid hydrogenated fats, processed foods, white flour, and sugar.

What Is the Highest Level of Carbohydrates That I Can Consume in the Fourth Phase of the Atkins Diet?

You must remember to identify your carbohydrate tolerance and balance to help you maintain your ideal weight. You should introduce more carbohydrates to your diet by slowly increasing your intake until you are no longer experiencing weight gain. You must also ensure that you can control your cravings and weight. Every person has an individual carbohydrate tolerance, and it is important that you use some trial and error methods to identify your tolerance.

Chapter 7: Atkins Diet Food List

As discussed in the previous chapter, the traditional Atkins diet has four phases. You can cut back on your intake of carbohydrates in every phase, but you will need to control this the most when you are in the first phase of the Atkins diet. You can choose to switch to the Atkins 40 and Atkins 100 diet plans. Your intake of carbohydrates will be higher when you follow the Atkins 40 and Atkins 100 plans, but you will still be consuming fewer carbohydrates than the amount recommended by the USDA. Regardless of the phase you want to follow or the version of the plan you choose, you must plan your meals around your fat and protein intake. You must reduce your intake of carbohydrates and keep the quantity within the suggested limits.

There are different lists of food that you can consume for the Atkins 20, Atkins 40, and Atkins 100 diet plans. These sections will cover the list of foods that you can and cannot eat if you follow the Atkins 20 diet. You can eat some of these foods if you choose to follow the Atkins 40 diet, but only in limited amounts. When you follow the Atkins 100 diet, you do not have to avoid consuming any of these foods. You will only need to maintain your carbohydrate intake to 50 grams a day.

Foods You Can Eat

Foundational Vegetables

When you follow the Atkins diet, you will need to reduce your intake of carbohydrates. You will need to consume vegetables and most of your carbohydrates should come from vegetables. It is important that you know how many carbohydrates you will be consuming when you eat a vegetable. You will need to consume at least 15 grams of carbs every day by eating vegetables like zucchini, mushrooms, spinach, tomatoes, asparagus, and broccoli.

Shellfish and Fish

When you are on the Atkins diet, you should consume no more than 4 ounces of fish per day. You should not consume breaded fish because you will be increasing your intake of carbohydrates. Types of fish including sardines, tuna, flounder, cod, halibut, and salmon are allowed. You can also consume shellfish like clams, shrimp, and lobster. Mussels and oysters are also okay to consume, but you will need to limit your intake since these shellfish are rich in carbs.

Poultry

The Atkins diet instructs you to divide your intake of protein between 3 different meals. It is also important that you obtain your protein from a variety of sources. You can consume goose, pheasant, chicken, turkey, and duck, and limit your servings to 6 ounces per day.

Meat

Only consume 4 ounces of meat per day. You can consume venison, veal, lamb, pork, and beef since those are the only meats that adhere to the rules of the Atkins diet.

When you follow the Atkins diet, you will need to be very careful about certain types of meat, including ham, bacon, and other processed meats. These types of meat will contain extra sugar since they are often cured with sugar alone. If you follow the Atkins diet, you will need to avoid the different meat cold cuts and also avoid meat that is stored with nitrates.

Eggs, Cheese, and Cream

When you follow the Atkins diet, it is recommended that you consume eggs since they are rich in protein. Cheese is rich in carbohydrates, but you must ensure that you consume no more than 3 ounces of cheese per day. You can consume some dairy products like cream and sour cream, but it is advised that you do not consume yogurt, goat's milk, ricotta cheese, and cottage cheese.

Fats and Oils

There is a popular myth that people who follow the Atkins diet consume large amounts of added fats like butter, but this is not true. If you follow the Atkins diet, you must ensure that you maintain your fat intake to 4 tablespoons per day. You can consume fats like mayonnaise, butter, walnut oil, sesame oil, and mayonnaise.

Foods You Cannot Eat or Should Only Eat Sparingly

Grains and Grain Products

There is a wide range of foods made from grains that are a part of the standard American diet. You cannot consume these foods during the first phase of the Atkins diet. These foods include pasta, bread, muffins, cereal, baked goods, and bagels. You should also avoid grains like oats, barley, and rice. When you move to the next phases of the Atkins diet, you must learn to limit the grains in your diet. You must ensure that you choose whole grains that are rich in fiber.

Fruits and Fruit Juice

Fruits and fruit juices provide a lot of important vitamins and minerals. That being said, these foods also contain sugars like fructose, and it is for this reason that they are rich in carbohydrates. You can add a few low-carb fruits to your diet starting from the second phase of the Atkins diet, but you will need to avoid them during the first phase.

Beans and Legumes

Beans and legumes like split peas, garbanzo beans, and kidney beans are a great source of nutrients. These foods are also rich in carbohydrates, and it is for this reason that you will need to avoid them in most of the phases of the Atkins 20 diet.

Alcoholic Beverages

During the first phase of the Atkins diet, you will need to avoid consuming alcohol completely. You can begin to consume alcohol in moderation when you enter the second phase of the

Atkins diet. Mixers for cocktails often have more sugar when compared to clear liquors.

Sugary Beverages

Most non-alcoholic beverages are made using artificial sweeteners or sugar. It is important to remember that sugary beverages are off limits, especially those that are prepared with artificial sweeteners like sucralose, stevia, or saccharin. If you still want to consume these beverages, you must ensure that your intake of sugar is limited to the equivalent of 3 packets of sugar a day.

Nuts and Seeds

Other good sources of proteins and fats are nuts and seeds. These foods also contain carbohydrates, which will increase your daily intake. It is advised that you do not consume these foods when you follow the Atkins diet, particularly during the induction phase. If you choose to stay in the induction phase for longer than two weeks, you can swap at least 3 grams of carbohydrates that you obtain from vegetables with nuts and seeds.

Sauces, Salad Dressings, and Condiments

There are many salad dressings and sauces that are made using fat, and some of these also contain sugar. For instance, barbecue sauce and ketchup are rich in sugar. Salad dressings can also add excess sugar to your food. It is for this reason that these products are off limits. You can consume these foods if they contain natural sugars.

Junk Foods and Sweets

Any empty calorie food or processed junk food that is made from sugar or starch should be avoided. Some savory foods like pizza and French fries also contain some sugar, and it is for this reason that these foods should be avoided by people following the Atkins diet.

Recommended Timing

The Atkins diet has been structured based on the amount of weight you need to lose to reach your ideal weight. The diet has also been structured based on the plan that you choose to adopt. Your progress and the plan you choose to follow will determine the amount of time you will need to spend on each phase of the Atkins diet.

Ideally, the first phase of the diet, the induction phase, should only last for two weeks. As the person following the diet, you can choose to continue the phase for a longer period as long as your body is able to adapt well to the change. If you have too much weight to lose, you may need to stay in the induction phase for a longer period. You must ensure that you limit your intake of carbohydrates to only 20 grams a day. This will ensure that your body automatically shifts into the state of ketosis. You can move into the second phase when you are nearing your ideal weight.

During the third phase, you will need to work on tuning your diet. You can include different foods in your diet, but you will need to ensure that the new food that you have added to your diet does not increase your weight. You can continue to stay in this phase until you have maintained your ideal weight for at least a month. This phase will help you design the ideal meal plan that you will need to follow for life.

The Atkins 40 diet plan is for people who need or want to lose 40 pounds or less. Women who are pregnant or breastfeeding can also choose to follow this diet plan if they have the right guidance. You will need to consume three meals a day when you follow this, and also consume about 10 grams of carbohydrates during each meal. You can also consume two snacks a day that have around 5 grams of carbohydrates each.

The Atkins 100 diet was designed for people who are only looking at maintaining their weight. This program was designed for people who want to develop a lifelong eating style. When you follow this diet, you are allowed to consume three meals a day, where each meal should contain 25 grams of carbohydrates. You can also consume snacks twice a day, and each snack can consist of 10 grams of carbohydrates.

Resources and Tips

There is a lot of information that you can find on the Internet about the Atkins diet. You can also choose to sign up for different Atkins meal kits or any paid plan. These plans range anywhere between $75 to $100. These meal kits will also give you some other resources and tools that will help you stick to your plan.

If you know how to cook a low-carb diet based on the Atkins-compliant foods at home, you will be successful. Most people find it difficult to stick to a plan indefinitely, so if you choose to stick to the Atkins diet for life, it is important that you learn the necessary skills that will help you maintain your eating style right from the start. There are many recipes that are available on the Internet and in this book. The recipes mentioned in this book are some of the most delicious Atkins-friendly recipes you will find.

Adjusting to Ketosis

If you are following the Atkins 20 diet, you will also need to be prepared for some of the side effects that you will notice during the first phase of the diet. When you do not give your body the required amount of carbohydrates, it will turn towards the stored fat and burn it to provide your body with sufficient energy. This switch will definitely affect your body. Your body will automatically switch to the metabolic state called ketosis when you begin to follow the Atkins diet.

When your body is in the state of ketosis because of the Atkins diet or other low-carb diets, you may experience constipation, mood swings, bad breath, fatigue, nausea, and high levels of calcium excretion or kidney stones. You will have bad breath because the ketones from your body will be expelled through your lungs. If you wish to prevent these side effects, you must drink water frequently. You should also stay active and avoid skipping meals.

When you follow the Atkins 40 and Atkins 100 diets, you will experience only some of these symptoms because of a less dramatic decrease in your intake of carbohydrates. You can reduce these symptoms by drinking the necessary amount of water.

Modifications

If you are a vegetarian or a vegan, you can choose to follow the Eco Atkins diet if you are interested in following the Atkins diet. This program was developed in Toronto by a group of researchers in the St. Michael's Hospital. This diet has a similar ratio of carbs and protein as the original Atkins diet, but it replaces animal fats with vegetarian protein. This diet is recommended for both vegetarians and vegans.

If you are someone who wants to follow a gluten-free diet, you can find different options in the Atkins diet. The Atkins diet provides not only gluten-free recipes, but also offers different gluten-free products. The Atkins induction phase will make you reduce your intake of carbohydrates, unlike any other low-carb diet. These diets will also lead to weight loss. You can start following the Atkins diet by following all the rules of the induction phase of the Atkins diet. You can loosen up a little bit if you find that you are on the verge of quitting the diet altogether.

Chapter 8: How to Ease into the Atkins Diet

The Atkins diet is one of the best ways to lose weight, feel great about yourself, and improve your lifestyle and eating habits. Now that you have learned a lot about the Atkins diet, you are a step closer to beginning your journey and sticking to the diet plan that you create for yourself. You must, however, ensure that you dive in slowly. This chapter provides some tips that you can use to start your diet in a healthy manner. You should remember to never jump right into the diet since that will make it hard for you to stick to your plan.

Set Goals

It is important that you create a plan and set healthy and achievable goals before you begin the diet. This is an important step to ensuring that you adhere to your Atkins program or any other dietary program. You must always keep the bigger picture in mind if you want to stay motivated and on track. This big picture is your goal, and when you keep it in mind, you will work towards it. You can also write your goals down and leave them in places where you can view them. This will work as a positive reminder.

Determine the Right Atkins Plan for You

There are different Atkins plans that you can choose for yourself, and you can identify the right plan for you by taking different surveys on the Internet. These plans will help you define which phase of the Atkins diet you will need to begin with. For instance, if you choose the Atkins 20 plan, you will need to start with the induction phase. As mentioned earlier, the purpose of this phase is to shift your body's metabolism to a point where your body will begin to burn the stored fat and not the carbohydrates that you consume. Your aim should be to set your carbohydrate intake to only 20 grams a day.

If you choose to stick to the Atkins 40 plan, you will need to consume 40 grams of carbohydrates every day. As you approach your ideal weight, you will need to increase your intake of carbohydrates if you wish to maintain your momentum.

Only Keep the Approved Foods at Home

There is a list of foods that are approved for each phase of the Atkins diet. Before you begin your diet, you must read through the approved list of foods that you can consume during each phase of the Atkins diet. This has been covered earlier in the book. You must familiarize yourself with the food lists and ensure that you stay on track. If you want to maintain your intake of carbohydrates, it is important that you measure your intake using a carb counter.

Plan Your Meals Using the Atkins Recipes

It is always a good idea to plan your meals in advance so you can save time during the week. This will also help you maintain your intake of carbohydrates. There are different recipes mentioned later in this book that you can use to plan your shopping. You can use the recipes mentioned to organize your meal plan for the week. When you enjoy the meals that you are cooking, you will find it easier to stick to the required macro intake.

Stay Hydrated

You should drink a lot of water and keep yourself hydrated. When you are hydrated, you can prevent any electrolyte imbalances caused due to the loss of water weight in the first phase of the Atkins diet. You should try to drink at least 8 glasses of water every day, and you can replace at least 4 of these glasses with green tea, coffee, or chicken, vegetable, or beef broth.

Never Avoid Fats

You may be worried about how consuming fats is going to help you lose weight. It may seem counterproductive to you, but it is important for you to consume healthy fats if you want to lose weight while following the Atkins diet. When you consume the required amount of healthy fats in your diet, your body can absorb vitamins better. This will help keep you healthy and also heighten your tastes so you will enjoy your meals even more.

Snack Frequently

You are allowed and, in fact, encouraged to consume snacks when you are on the Atkins diet. You can consume two snacks every day between breakfast, lunch, and dinner. This will ensure that you are not frequently hungry and that you can fight any carb cravings. You can keep some protein bars or health bars with you to fight off any hunger pangs.

Surround Yourself with Motivation and Support

You must always find a way to stay motivated and accountable when you are on the Atkins diet. You can choose to start the Atkins diet with your friends, family, or even with a friend who is already a part of the Atkins community. You will find it easier to manage your weight loss goals when you surround yourself with people who can support your low-carb diet and lifestyle, and motivate you to stick to your diet plan.

Now, let's take a look at some recipes that you can use to create a plan for yourself.

Chapter 9: Atkins Recipes — Phase 1 (Induction)

Chocolate Slush

Servings: 1

Ingredients:

- ½ cup heavy cream
- 1 tablespoon unsweetened cocoa powder
- ½ teaspoon vanilla extract
- ¼ cup water
- ¼ cup sugar-free chocolate syrup

Directions:

1. Add cream, cocoa powder, water, and chocolate syrup to a saucepan.

2. Place the saucepan over medium heat. When it begins to boil, lower the heat and simmer for 3-4 minutes while stirring occasionally. Remove from heat.

3. Add vanilla, mix well, and cool completely before pouring into an ice cube tray and freezing until nearly firm.

4. Remove the ice cubes from the tray and add into the food processor bowl. Blend until slush texture is obtained, then serve in a glass.

Shakshuka

Servings: 8

Ingredients:

- 2 tablespoons extra-virgin olive oil
- 1 small onion, diced
- 2 red bell peppers, sliced
- 3 garlic cloves, minced
- 2 large cans crushed tomatoes
- 1 can diced tomatoes
- 1 tablespoon tomato paste
- 2 teaspoons harissa
- 2 teaspoons cumin
- 1 teaspoon paprika
- ½ teaspoon coriander

- ½ teaspoon red pepper flakes
- A pinch of salt
- A pinch of freshly ground pepper
- 8 large eggs
- ½ cup feta
- Freshly chopped parsley
- Sliced bread for serving

Directions:

1. Preheat the oven to 375° Fahrenheit while warming some oil in a large skillet.

2. Add diced onions and cook them over medium heat until properly caramelized (about 20 minutes). Then, add the bell peppers and cook for 5 minutes.

3. Add garlic, diced and crushed tomatoes, tomato paste, harissa, and spices and mix well. Cook for another 10 minutes.

4. Sprinkle salt and pepper on top and allow the mixture to simmer for about 10 minutes before transferring to a baking pan.

5. Gently make about 8 wells in the pan, crack each egg into a well, and season with some salt and pepper.

6. Cover with aluminum foil and bake for 15 minutes until egg whites are set, not brown.

7. Garnish with parsley and feta and serve alongside some warm bread.

Peppermint Hot Chocolate

Servings: 2

Ingredients:

- 1 cup unsweetened almond milk
- 2 Atkins chocolate mint bars, chopped
- 4 tablespoons unsweetened cocoa powder
- Whipped cream to top (optional)
- Sweetener like stevia or erythritol to taste

Directions:

1. Place a saucepan over medium heat.
2. Add milk and cocoa powder and whisk until well incorporated.

3. Add sweetener and chocolate bar. Stir constantly until chocolate melts.

4. Pour into cups and serve immediately. Top with whipped cream if using.

Cajun Tofu

Servings: 6-8

Ingredients:

- 4 teaspoons Cajun seasoning
- 2 tablespoons olive oil
- 2 packages (14.5 ounces each) extra-firm tofu, cut into thick slices
- Mixed salad greens to serve

Directions:

1. Sprinkle about half of the Cajun seasoning at the bottom of a baking dish.

2. Place the tofu slices in the dish. Sprinkle remaining Cajun seasoning on top.

3. Cover the dish with cling wrap and let it marinate for 7-8 hours.

4. Place a nonstick skillet over medium heat. Add a teaspoon of oil. Place the tofu slices in the pan and cook until the underside is golden brown.

5. Flip sides and cook the other side until golden brown.

6. Repeat steps 4-5 and cook the remaining tofu slices.

7. Place the browned tofu over a bed of salad greens and serve.

Beef Huevos Rancheros Over Canadian Bacon

Servings: 2

Ingredients:

- 3 ounces 80% lean ground beef
- ⅛ teaspoon garlic powder
- ⅛ teaspoon ground cumin
- Salt to taste
- ½ teaspoon chili powder
- ⅛ teaspoon dried oregano
- Pepper to taste

- ¼ cup canned green chili peppers
- 2 slices Canadian bacon
- ¼ cup shredded cheddar cheese
- 2 large eggs
- A handful fresh cilantro, chopped
- A little oil or butter to grease

Directions:

1. Place a skillet over medium heat. Add a little butter or oil. When the butter melts, add beef and sauté until brown. Break it apart as it cooks.
2. Add chilies, oregano, and spices and cook for 4-5 minutes. Turn off the heat. Place the bacon slices on top of the beef.
3. Place another skillet over medium heat. Add a little butter. When butter melts, add eggs and scramble them. Cook until the eggs are the desired doneness (soft or firm).
4. To assemble: place a slice of bacon on each serving plate. Divide the beef mixture and place over the bacon. Divide the eggs and place over the beef.
5. Garnish with cheese and cilantro and serve.

Omelet-Stuffed Peppers

Servings: 4

Ingredients

- 2 large bell peppers
- 8 large eggs
- ¼ cup milk
- 4 slices bacon
- 1 cup cheddar cheese, shredded
- 2 tablespoons chopped chives
- A pinch of kosher salt
- Some freshly cracked pepper

Directions:

1. Preheat the oven to 400° F.

2. Wash the bell peppers thoroughly under running water and pat dry using paper towels. Using a sharp knife, halve them and remove the seeds.

3. Place the halved peppers on a baking tray and bake them for 5 minutes.

4. In a bowl, add the eggs and milk and beat together using a fork.

5. Gently stir in some chives, cheese, bacon, salt, and pepper and whisk again.

6. Once the peppers are completely baked, pour the egg mixture gently into the peppers.

7. Place them back in the oven for about 40 minutes until the eggs are slightly golden.

8. Garnish with chives on top and serve immediately.

Scrambled Eggs with Herbs

Servings: 1

Ingredients:

- 3 large eggs
- Salt and pepper to taste
- ½ teaspoon minced fresh parsley
- ½ teaspoon minced fresh tarragon
- ½ teaspoon minced chives
- 1 tablespoon heavy cream

- ½ tablespoon unsalted butter

Directions:

1. Add eggs, cream, salt, pepper, tarragon, and parsley into a bowl and whisk well.

2. Place a nonstick skillet over medium heat and add butter. When the butter melts, add the egg mixture.

3. Do not stir for a minute. Then, scramble mixture with a wooden spoon. When the eggs are cooked to a soft, curd-like consistency, remove from heat and serve.

Low-Carb Breakfast Muffins

Servings: 12

Ingredients:

- 12 ham slices
- 1 cup cheddar cheese
- 12 large eggs
- A pinch of kosher salt
- ½ teaspoon ground black pepper

Directions:

1. Preheat the oven to 400° Fahrenheit.

2. Grease muffin tin with butter and line each cup with cheddar and a slice of ham.

3. Gently crack an egg into each muffin cup and season with salt and pepper.

4. Bake muffins for 15 minutes, cool for 5 minutes, garnish with parsley, and serve.

Almond Pancakes

Servings: 8

Ingredients:

- 11.3-ounce package of almond meal
- ½ cup milk
- 6 eggs
- ½ teaspoon baking powder
- ½ teaspoon Splenda
- 2 tablespoons butter to fry pancakes
- ½ teaspoon salt
- ½ teaspoon ground cinnamon

- ¼ teaspoon ground nutmeg
- ¼ teaspoon vanilla extract

Directions:

1. Whisk together all the ingredients (except butter) in a bowl.

2. Place a pan over medium heat. Add about 1 teaspoon butter to pan. When butter melts, add about ¼ cup of the batter in the pan. Swirl the pan around so that the batter spreads slightly.

3. In a couple of minutes, bubbles will appear on top of the pancake. Cook until the underside is golden brown. Flip sides and cook the other side.

4. Remove onto a plate.

5. Repeat steps 2-4 and make pancakes with the remaining batter.

Sausage and Cauliflower Bake

Servings: 3

Ingredients:

- 1 small cauliflower, cut into florets

- 3 pork sausages
- ½ teaspoon salt
- Pepper to taste
- 4 tablespoons cream cheese
- 3 slices Gruyere cheese

Directions:

1. Preheat oven to 350° Fahrenheit.
2. Add cauliflower to a pot with a cup of water. Place the pot over medium heat. Cook until cauliflower is soft, then discard most of the water.
3. Mash cauliflower with a potato masher.
4. Add cream cheese, salt, and pepper.
5. Place a nonstick skillet over medium heat. Add sausages and cook until brown. Remove from heat.
6. Remove sausage and place on your cutting board. When cool enough to handle, slice the sausages.
7. Add sausage to cauliflower mash and mix well.
8. Add half of the cauliflower mixture into a greased baking dish and spread evenly.

9. Place half the cheese slices over the mixture.

10. Spread the remaining cauliflower mixture over the cheese slices.

11. Place the remaining cheese slices over the cauliflower layer.

12. Bake for 30 minutes, then serve.

Sheet Pan Brussels Sprouts and Egg and Bacon Hash

Servings: 6

Ingredients:

- 6 lbs. trimmed and halved Brussels sprouts
- 6 large slices of bacon
- 2 tablespoons extra virgin olive oil
- 2 tablespoons Buffalo sauce
- ½ teaspoon garlic powder
- Pinch of red pepper flakes
- ½ teaspoon black pepper
- ½ teaspoon salt

- 6 large eggs

- Some chopped chives for garnishing

Directions:

1. Preheat the oven to 425° Fahrenheit.

2. In a bowl, combine Brussels sprouts, bacon, olive oil, Buffalo sauce, garlic powder, and red pepper flakes and mix well.

3. Spread mixture across a large baking sheet and bake until bacon is crispy.

4. Use a large wooden spoon to make 6 nests in the hash and then gently crack an egg into each of these holes.

5. Season with salt and pepper.

6. Bake the eggs for about 10 minutes until they are nicely done.

7. Garnish with some chopped chives and buffalo sauce and serve.

Low-Carb Sausage Breakfast

Servings: 3

Ingredients:

- 6 large eggs
- 2 tablespoons heavy cream
- A pinch of red pepper flakes
- A pinch of kosher salt
- Some freshly ground black pepper
- 1 tablespoon butter
- 3 slices cheddar cheese
- 6 frozen sausage patties
- 1 large avocado, sliced

Directions:

1. In a bowl, crack the eggs, add heavy cream and red pepper flakes and beat them together.
2. Add some salt and pepper and whisk well using a fork.
3. Heat a large skillet on medium heat. Pour one third of the batter over the skillet and gently place a slice of cheese on top.
4. Add a bit of butter on top and allow the batter to cook

properly for about 1-2 minutes.

5. Add 2 sausage patties in the middle of the egg batter and fold it using a spatula.

6. Add a slice of avocado on top and serve.

7. Repeat this process with the rest of the batter.

Buffalo Chicken Wings

Servings: 3

Ingredients:

- 1 lb. of chicken wings with skin
- 1 small egg
- ½ teaspoon salt
- ¼ teaspoon pepper
- ⅛ teaspoon celery salt
- ¼ teaspoon garlic powder
- Red or cayenne pepper to taste
- ½ cup cider vinegar
- ¼ cup canola oil

For dip:

- 8 tablespoons Atkins diet-friendly mayonnaise
- 1 small scallion or spring onion, sliced
- ¼ cup sour cream
- 3 tablespoons crumbled blue cheese or Roquefort cheese
- 1 small clove garlic, minced
- 1 tablespoon lemon juice

Directions:

1. Preheat oven to 450° Fahrenheit.
2. Set aside the chicken, add other ingredients to a bowl, and whisk well.
3. Grease a baking dish with a little oil.
4. Place chicken in a bowl and coat it with the mixture. Remove the chicken pieces and shake to remove excess mixture.
5. Place chicken pieces in the prepared baking dish and bake for about 30 minutes or until crisp. Turn the chicken pieces a few times while baking. Baste with the marinade

each time you turn the chicken.

6. Meanwhile, add all the ingredients for dip into a bowl and whisk well.

7. Cover and set aside to let the flavors set in.

8. Serve crispy chicken wings with dip.

Crustless Pumpkin and Ham Quiche

Servings: 4

Ingredients:

- 1 small onion, chopped
- 2 large eggs
- ½ cup cooked, mashed pumpkin
- ½ tablespoon chopped parsley
- Cayenne pepper to taste
- Salt to taste
- 1 tablespoon unsalted butter + extra to grease
- ¼ cup heavy cream
- ¼ cup cured, roasted ham

- ½ cup shredded Gruyere cheese
- Freshly ground pepper to taste

Directions:

1. Preheat oven to 350° Fahrenheit.
2. Grease a small pie plate with a little oil or butter.
3. Place a skillet over medium heat. Add butter. When butter melts, add onion and sauté until translucent.
4. Add eggs into a bowl and whisk well. Add cream and whisk well.
5. Add the rest of the ingredients and whisk well.
6. Spoon into pie plate and bake for about 30 minutes, or until the center is firm.
7. Remove from the oven and cool before serving.

Low-Carb Mushroom Omelet

Servings: 1

Ingredients:

- 3 large eggs
- 1 ounce of butter, for frying

- 1 ounce of cheese, shredded
- 1 small yellow onion
- 3 mushrooms
- A pinch of salt
- A pinch of pepper

Directions:

1. Wash the mushrooms properly under some running water and pat them dry using paper towels. Using a sharp knife, gently slice them and set them aside.

2. In a bowl, crack the eggs and mix them with some salt and pepper. Whisk the eggs with a fork until the mixture is nicely blended.

3. Sprinkle some salt and pepper on top.

4. Melt some butter on a pan on low heat and add egg batter on top.

5. Once the omelet begins to cook, allow it to get slightly firmer.

6. Sprinkle some cheese and mushrooms on top. Add the onion slices on top of the mushroom slices.

7. Use a spatula to gently ease the edges of the omelet and fold it over.

8. Omelet will start to turn golden brown. Once this happens, remove from heat and slide it onto a large plate.

9. Season with some pepper and serve.

Red Cabbage Slaw with Mustard Vinaigrette

Servings: 3-4

Ingredients:

- ½ teaspoon lemon zest, grated
- ¾ lbs. red cabbage, shredded

For dressing:

- ¼ cup rice vinegar
- 1 ½ tablespoons granulated sweetener
- ½ teaspoon minced onion
- 2 tablespoons olive oil
- ½ tablespoon mustard
- Salt to taste

Directions:

1 Add all the ingredients for dressing into a bowl and whisk well.

2 Add cabbage and toss well.

3 Cover the bowl with plastic wrap and refrigerate for a couple of hours.

4 Sprinkle lemon zest on top and serve.

Beef and Broccoli Stir Fry

Servings: 4-5

Ingredients:

- lbs. beef, top steak, cut into ¼ inch slices
- 14-16 ounces broccoli, cut into florets, slice the stalk into thin strips
- 4 cloves garlic, minced
- tablespoons minced fresh ginger
- ¼ cup water
- red chili peppers, minced
- 2 teaspoons crushed red pepper flakes

- tablespoons apple cider vinegar
- tablespoons canola oil
- 4 tablespoons soy sauce
- 3 cups beef broth
- 2 tablespoons sesame seeds
- Salt to taste
- Pepper to taste

Directions:

1. Add beef, soy sauce, and garlic into a bowl and mix well. Let it sit for 15-20 minutes.
2. Add broth, vinegar, red pepper flakes, and ginger root and mix well.
3. Place a large, nonstick skillet over medium-high heat. Add 2 tablespoons oil. When oil is heated, add beef and cook until browned. Remove from the pan and set aside.
4. Place the pan back on heat. Add remaining oil. When oil is heated, add broccoli and chili peppers and sauté for a minute.

5. Add water, cover, and cook until broccoli is tender and bright green in color. Stir frequently. Add salt and pepper to taste.

6. Add sauce mixture and cooked beef. Simmer for 3-4 minutes.

7. Remove from heat. Sprinkle with sesame seeds and serve.

Asian Steak Salad

Servings: 4

Ingredients:

- 2 cloves garlic, peeled and finely chopped
- 2-inch piece of ginger, peeled and grated
- 2 tablespoons tamari
- 1 teaspoon sesame oil
- 16 ounces beef top sirloin, trimmed of fat
- ½ tablespoon vegetable oil
- 4 large scallions, finely chopped
- 2 medium red sweet peppers, cut into ¼ inch thin

strips

- 1 tablespoon unseasoned rice wine vinegar
- ½ teaspoon zero calorie sweetener
- ½ teaspoon curry powder
- 10 ounces baby spinach
- Salt to taste
- Pepper to taste

Directions:

1. Add garlic, ginger, sesame oil, tamari, sweetener, vinegar, and green onion into a bowl. Mix well. Transfer half this mixture into a zip lock bag. Set the remaining mixture aside.

2. Dry the steak by patting with paper towels. Place on your cutting board. Cut the steak into slices of about ⅛ inch.

3. Add into the zip lock bag. Turn the bag around to coat the steak. Chill for 2-3 hours.

4. Place a skillet over medium-high heat. Add vegetable oil. When the oil is heated, add only steak (not the

marinade) and cook for about 3 minutes.

5. Remove beef with a slotted spoon and place in a bowl. Add spinach, red pepper, and the mixture that was set aside. Toss well. Season with salt and pepper and serve.

Beef Bolognese with Parmesan

Servings: 4

Ingredients

- 2 ounces shallots
- 3 tablespoons olive oil
- 2 large stalks celery, sliced
- 2 Roma tomatoes, chopped into 1-inch pieces
- 10.75 ounce can of tomato sauce
- 2 tablespoons balsamic vinegar
- 2 cloves garlic, peeled and finely chopped
- 2 medium zucchinis, cut into ½-inch cubes
- 2 heads cos or romaine lettuce, torn into 1-inch pieces
- 28 ounces 85% lean ground beef

- 1 teaspoon Italian seasoning
- 4 tablespoons grated Parmesan cheese
- Salt to taste
- Pepper to taste

Directions:

1. Dry the beef with paper towels.
2. Place a skillet over medium heat. Add 1 tablespoon oil. When the oil is heated, add shallot and garlic and cook until onion turns translucent.
3. Stir in the beef and cook until light brown. Break it apart as it cooks. Drain extra fat from the pan.
4. Stir in Italian seasoning and tomato sauce and mix well. Lower heat and cook for 8 to 10 minutes.
5. Stir in the celery and zucchini and cook until tender.
6. Put lettuce and tomatoes in a large bowl. Add vinegar, salt, pepper, and remaining oil and toss well.
7. Divide beef into bowls. Garnish with Parmesan cheese and serve with lettuce and tomato salad.

Baked Salmon with Bok Choy

Servings: 4

Ingredients:

- 24 ounces boneless raw salmon, patted dry
- 12 ounces mushrooms (preferably shiitake), quartered
- Salt to taste
- Pepper to taste
- 4 tablespoons tamari
- Juice of 2 lemons
- 3 heads Chinese cabbage or bok choy
- 1 tablespoon butter
- 3 tablespoons olive oil

Directions:

1. Preheat oven to 350° Fahrenheit.
2. Mix tamari and lemon juice in a bowl. Set aside half of the mixture.
3. Sprinkle salt and pepper over the salmon and place in

the remaining tamari mixture. Chill for 15 minutes.

4. Line a baking sheet with foil. Add butter and 2 tablespoons oil on the baking sheet.

5. Place in the oven until butter melts, then remove the baking sheet from the oven.

6. Lay the salmon on the baking sheet and bake for about 10 minutes, or until salmon flakes easily when pierced with a fork. Remove from oven and keep warm.

7. Place a large nonstick pan over medium-high heat. Add remaining oil. When the oil is heated, stir in mushrooms and bok choy and cook until tender.

8. Add the tamari mixture that was set aside and mix well. Remove from heat.

9. To serve: divide the bok choy mixture among 4 plates and top with salmon.

Balsamic Pork Loin with Roasted Rosemary Cauliflower

Servings: 4

Ingredients:

- 24 ounces pork tenderloin, patted dry

- 1 teaspoon dried rosemary

- 1 teaspoon pepper

- 1 teaspoon salt

- 1 teaspoon garlic powder

- 6 teaspoons dried mustard

- ¼ teaspoon ground allspice

- 24 ounces cauliflower

- 4 tablespoons balsamic vinegar

- 4 tablespoons olive oil

Directions:

1. Preheat oven to 350° Fahrenheit.

2. Add spices, salt, vinegar, and olive oil into a bowl and

whisk well.

3. Place pork in a large zip lock bag. Pour the vinegar mixture in the bag. Seal the bag and turn the bag to coat the pork well.

4. Chill until use.

5. Add cauliflower to a bowl. Sprinkle rosemary and a little salt and toss well.

6. Spread the cauliflower on a baking sheet lined with foil.

7. Roast in oven for about 25 minutes, or until light brown.

8. Remove the baking sheet from the oven and keep the cauliflower warm.

9. Transfer the pork and marinade into a baking dish.

10. Roast in oven for 12-14 minutes, or until cooked through.

11. Divide the cauliflower equally and place on 4 plates. Put pork on top. Drizzle with cooked juices and serve.

Coconut Blondies

Servings: 12

Ingredients:

- ½ cup coconut flour
- ⅓ cup coconut oil, melted
- 3 large eggs
- ¼ cup cream
- 2 teaspoons vanilla extract
- ¼ cup powdered sweetener
- 1 teaspoon baking powder
- ¼ cup dried coconut
- Some coconut flakes for garnish

Directions:

1. Preheat the oven to 350° Fahrenheit.
2. Line a baking tray with parchment paper.
3. In a large bowl, add the eggs, vanilla extract, coconut oil, and coconut cream and mix well.

4. In another bowl, add dried coconut, coconut flour, sweetener, and baking powder and mix well. Use a large spoon to mix the batter well so there are no lumps. You can add some more sweetener if you would like.

5. Pour this entire mixture into the baking pan.

6. Bake for about 20 minutes or until all the eggs turn slightly brown.

7. Allow the blondies to cool off before cutting them.

8. Serve immediately.

Chapter 10: Atkins Recipes — Phase 2 (Ongoing Weight Loss/Balancing)

Easy Pizza Eggs

Servings: 2

Ingredients:

- 1 tablespoon olive oil
- 2 large eggs
- A pinch of kosher salt
- Some freshly ground pepper
- ¼ cup pizza sauce, divided
- ¼ cup shredded mozzarella cheese, divided
- 10 mini pepperonis
- Some freshly grated parmesan, for garnish
- Some dried oregano, for garnish
- 1 mason jar lid

Directions:

1. Spray skillet with some cooking spray and heat it on medium flame.

2. Place a mason jar lid at the center of the skillet.

3. Gently crack an egg inside the jar.

4. Top it up with some cheese, pepperoni and pizza sauce.

5. Cover it with a lid. Allow the egg white to cook completely and until the cheese is completely melted. This could take about 5 minutes.

6. Repeat the same process with the remaining ingredients.

7. Transfer to a large plate, garnish with some oregano, Parmesan, pepper, and salt, and serve immediately.

California Breakfast Burrito

Servings: 2

Ingredients:

- 2 low-carb tortillas
- 3 small scallions or spring onions, sliced
- 1 small tomato, chopped

- 4 large eggs

- A handful fresh cilantro, chopped

- ½ tablespoon canola oil

- 2 ounces canned green chili peppers

- Salt to taste

- Cayenne pepper to taste

- 2 tablespoons tomatillo salsa

- Pepper to taste

- ¼ cup shredded cheddar cheese

Directions:

1. Place a nonstick skillet over medium-high flame. Add oil. When the oil is heated, stir in the tomato, scallions, and chilies, and sauté for a minute.

2. Season with salt and pepper and cook for about 2 minutes.

3. Move the vegetable mixture to one side of the pan.

4. Pour eggs in the center of the skillet. Add cayenne pepper and stir. Cook until eggs are soft-cooked and

curd-like.

5. Bring the vegetables back to the center and mix well. Turn off the heat.

6. Warm the tortillas following the instructions on the package.

7. Place the tortillas on individual serving plates. Divide the scrambled mixture between the tortillas.

8. Garnish with tomatillo salsa, cilantro, and cheese.

9. Roll and serve.

Blackberry Smoothie

Servings: 2

Ingredients:

- ½ cup frozen blackberries
- 2 ounces vanilla whey protein
- ½ teaspoon ground cinnamon
- 1 teaspoon vanilla extract
- 2 cups coconut milk, unsweetened
- 2 tablespoons ground golden flaxseed meal

- ⅛ teaspoon ground allspice

Directions:

1. Add the ingredients to a blender and blend until smooth.

2. Pour into 2 glasses and serve.

Low-Carb Strawberry Popsicles

Servings: 4-5

Ingredients:

- 8 ounces frozen mango, diced
- 8 ounces strawberries, roughly chopped
- 1 cup Greek yogurt
- ½ cup whipping cream
- 1 teaspoon vanilla extract

Directions:

1. Put strawberry and mango slices in the blender and blend them until smooth.

2. Add Greek yogurt and vanilla extract and give the mixture a whisk.

3. Add whipping cream and whisk again until there are no lumps in the mixture.

4. Pour popsicle mixture into popsicle molds and refrigerate them for about 2-3 hours before serving.

Eggplant and Ricotta Rolls

Servings: 2-3

Ingredients:

- 1 large eggplant, sliced lengthwise into 4-6 slices
- ½ lb. whole milk ricotta cheese, crumbled
- ½ teaspoon salt
- 1 teaspoon pepper powder
- 2 tablespoons olive oil
- ½ teaspoon minced fresh oregano or any other herb of your choice

Directions:

1. Place eggplant slices on a baking sheet.
2. Brush slices with a little oil.
3. Place rack 3 inches away from the heating element in a

grill. Heat the grill to high heat for 5-6 minutes.

4. Meanwhile, mix together the rest of the ingredients.

5. Remove from grill and cool slightly.

6. Spread ricotta mixture on the grilled eggplant slices.

7. Roll the slices tightly and fasten with a toothpick. Sprinkle oregano on top.

8. Serve with a salad of your choice.

Easy Almond Butter Cookies

Servings: 25

Ingredients:

- 1 cup almond butter, melted
- ½ cup almond flour
- 8 drops of stevia
- 2 tablespoons sugar-free syrup
- 1 teaspoon powdered cinnamon
- About 1 small block of chocolate, unsweetened

Directions:

1. In a bowl, combine the melted butter with some stevia using a spoon. Make sure the consistency isn't too runny and is slightly dough-like.

2. Using the palms of your hands, roll the dough into 25 small chocolate balls.

3. In a double boiler, melt the chocolate block. You can even fill a vessel full of water, bring it to a boil, add the chocolate block to another vessel and melt it by holding it over boiling water. Make sure you are constantly stirring the chocolate while doing so.

4. Use a spoon to coat each of the chocolate balls with this mixture and place them on a parchment sheet. Set them in the fridge for about 20 minutes until they slightly harden and serve them.

5. You can store these chocolate balls in the refrigerator for about 2 weeks.

Almond and Coconut Flour Muffins

Serves: 2-4

Ingredients:

- ¼ cup almond meal flour

- 2 teaspoons swerve or any other sugar substitute
- ½ teaspoon baking powder
- 2 large eggs
- 2 tablespoons sour cream
- ¾ cup high-fiber coconut flour
- 1 teaspoon ground cinnamon
- ¼ teaspoon salt
- 2 teaspoon extra-virgin olive oil

Directions:

1. Add all the dry ingredients into a bowl and stir.
2. Add all the wet ingredients into another bowl and whisk well.
3. Pour wet ingredients into dry ingredients and mix until well incorporated.
4. Divide into 2 microwave-safe mugs.
5. Microwave on High for 1 minute.
6. Remove from the microwave and cool for a few minutes. Loosen the edges of the muffin with a knife if

required.

7. When cool enough to handle, slice and serve with butter.

Stuffed Bell Peppers

Servings: 8

Ingredients:

- 4 medium red bell peppers, stemmed, halved, deseeded
- 4 cloves garlic, crushed
- 1 red onion, chopped
- 7 ounces mushrooms, sliced
- 2.8 ounces canned or cooked cannellini beans
- 2 cups shredded silver beet
- 4.2 ounces zucchini, chopped
- 3.5 ounces green beans, chopped
- ¼ cup parsley, chopped
- 2 tablespoons olive oil
- 4 tomatoes, quartered

- 1 brown onion, chopped
- 2 tablespoons fresh basil, chopped
- Salt to taste
- Pepper to taste

Directions:

1. Preheat oven to 350° Fahrenheit.
2. Place bell pepper halves, tomatoes, and 2 cloves garlic on a lined baking sheet. Season with salt and pepper and sprinkle a little olive oil over it.
3. Bake for about 20 minutes. Remove bell peppers from the oven after 10 minutes. Set aside the roasted tomatoes and garlic.
4. Meanwhile, place a skillet over medium heat. Add 1 tablespoon oil. When oil is heated, add onions and sauté until onions are translucent.
5. Add the rest of the ingredients of the stuffing except parsley. Cook until vegetables are soft.
6. Add parsley and remove from heat. Fill the bell peppers with this mixture. Bake for 15 minutes.
7. Add remaining oil into a pan. Add brown onion and

sauté until translucent.

8. Add about ½ cup water and stir. Lower heat and simmer for 10 minutes or until tomatoes are soft.

9. Add basil, salt, and pepper and mix well.

10. Drizzle sauce over bell peppers and serve.

Chewy Cookies

Servings: 7-8

Ingredients:

- 1 ½ cups almond butter
- 2 large eggs
- ½ cup natural sweetener (preferably swerve)
- ½ cup unsweetened cocoa powder
- 1 teaspoon vanilla extract
- A pinch of salt

Directions:

1. Preheat the oven to 350° Fahrenheit.
2. Line a baking tray with some parchment paper.

3. In a bowl, combine the sweetener with eggs, almond butter, cocoa powder, vanilla extract, and salt and add it to a food processor. Whisk this mixture until it forms a nice dough.

4. Roll dough into 1-inch balls. Place them on the baking sheet and gently press them down using a fork.

5. Place the tray in the oven and bake them for 12 minutes. Allow them to cool off on the baking sheet for about 2-3 minutes.

6. You can serve them immediately or store them in an air-tight container for up to a week.

Citrus-Chili Shrimp

Servings: 3

Ingredients:

- ¾ pound shrimp

- 3 ½ tablespoons extra virgin olive oil

- 3 teaspoons grated orange zest

- ¼ teaspoon salt

- ⅛ teaspoon chili powder

- ½ tablespoon unsalted butter
- 3 tablespoons fresh orange juice
- 1 tablespoon fresh lime juice
- Crushed red pepper flakes to taste
- ⅛ teaspoon ground cumin

Directions:

1. Add 3 tablespoons oil, 1 ½ tablespoons orange juice, lime juice, orange zest, chili powder, salt, red pepper flakes, and cumin into a bowl. Mix well.
2. Mix in the shrimp. Set aside for 10 minutes.
3. Place a skillet over medium heat. Add butter and ½ tablespoon oil. When butter melts, remove shrimp from marinade and place in the skillet. Set aside the marinade.
4. Cook until shrimp turns pink. Turn sides after 2 minutes of cooking.
5. Remove onto a plate.
6. Pour the marinade that was set aside into the skillet. Also add remaining orange juice and bring to a boil. Boil for a minute.

7. Pour over the shrimp and serve.

Asparagus, Mushrooms, and Peas

Servings: 3

Ingredients

- 1 ½ tablespoons unsalted butter
- ½ teaspoon minced garlic
- 2 tablespoons cider vinegar
- ½ pound asparagus
- 1 tablespoon heavy cream
- Salt to taste
- 3 small scallions or spring onions
- 1.5 ounces Portobello mushroom caps
- ½ cup water
- ¼ cup green peas
- 4 basil leaves, torn
- Pepper to taste

Directions:

1. Place a skillet over medium-high heat. Add 1 tablespoon butter. When butter melts, add scallions and lower the heat to medium heat. Cook until scallion wilts.

2. Stir in the garlic and cook until fragrant.

3. Add ½ tablespoon butter. Stir in the mushrooms and cook until soft.

4. Stir in the vinegar and simmer for a couple of minutes.

5. Add asparagus and water and stir. When it begins to boil, lower the heat and cook until nearly tender.

6. Stir in the peas and simmer for a couple of minutes.

7. Add cream and stir. Cook until thick. Turn off the heat. Add salt and pepper to taste. Add basil and stir.

8. Transfer into a bowl. Garnish with Parmesan cheese and serve.

Low-Carb Donuts

Servings: 12 mini donuts

Ingredients:

- 2 large eggs
- ¼ cup almond flour
- ¼ teaspoon apple cider vinegar
- 1 teaspoon vanilla extract
- ½ tablespoon coconut flour
- ¼ teaspoon xanthan gum
- 1 teaspoon cinnamon
- 1 teaspoon baking powder
- ½ teaspoon baking soda
- ⅛ teaspoon sea salt
- Mini donut pan

For the cinnamon and sugar coating

- ¼ cup granulated erythritol
- 1 teaspoon ground cinnamon
- 1 ½ teaspoons melted ghee, or butter if not paleo

For the chocolate glaze

- 2 ounces sugar-free chocolate, melted

- 1 teaspoon coconut oil, melted
- 1 teaspoon monk fruit sweetener

Directions:

1. Preheat the oven to 350° Fahrenheit.
2. In a bowl, combine apple cider vinegar, eggs, and vanilla and whip until smooth.
3. In another bowl, combine the almond flour, xanthan gum, coconut flour, cinnamon, baking powder, baking soda, and salt and mix again. Now, slowly combine the dry ingredients with the wet ones and stir them properly using a large spoon.
4. Grease a mini donut pan and pour the batter into it carefully.
5. Bake them for about 15 minutes until they turn golden brown.
6. Serve them once cooled.

Chapter 11: Atkins Recipes — Phase 3 (Pre-Maintenance)

Atkins Low-Carb Wheat Bread

Servings: 8-9 slices

Ingredients:

- ½ cup vital wheat gluten
- 1 ¼ teaspoons active dry yeast
- 9 tablespoons lukewarm water
- 6 tablespoons soy flour
- 2 tablespoons wheat bran
- ¾ teaspoon baking powder
- ½ teaspoon salt
- ½ packet granular sugar substitute
- 1 ¼ tablespoons extra-light olive oil
- ¼ cup vanilla whey protein powder
- 2 tablespoons ground golden flaxseed meal

Directions:

1. Preheat oven to 350° Fahrenheit.

2. Add yeast and warm water in a mixing bowl and set aside for 5 minutes. The mixture should be frothy.

3. Mix together all the dry ingredients in a large bowl.

4. Add yeast-water mixture and oil. Use a spatula and mix well to form dough. Cover the bowl with cling wrap and set aside for about an hour, or until it doubles in size.

5. Remove the dough from the bowl using the spatula and place on the countertop. Punch the dough.

6. Place the dough into a small, greased bread pan. Cover the pan with cling wrap and let it sit for about 30 minutes. Remove the wrap.

7. Bake for about 30 minutes or until brown on top. Cool, slice, and serve.

Chicken Eggplant Casserole

Servings: 4

Ingredients:

- 6 small eggplant, cut into 1-inch cubes

- 3 tablespoons grated Parmesan
- ½ cup shredded cheddar cheese
- 2 green onions, chopped
- 1 ½ tablespoons unsalted butter, melted
- ½ teaspoon salt
- ½ teaspoon freshly ground pepper
- ¾ lb. cooked chicken breasts, diced
- 2-3 slices Atkins low-carb bread, torn
- 3 large eggs, beaten
- A handful fresh cilantro, chopped
- 1 ½ tablespoons sour cream
- ¼ teaspoon paprika
- Cooking spray

Directions:

1. Preheat oven to 350° Fahrenheit.
2. Grease a baking dish with cooking spray.
3. Place some water in a saucepan with a little salt. Place

over high heat. When it begins to boil, add eggplant, cover partially, and cook until tender. Drain, cool slightly, mash the eggplant lightly, and transfer to a large bowl.

4. Place the bread in a food processor and blend until fine crumbs are left. Add Parmesan and pulse until well mixed.

5. Add half the breadcrumb mixture to the eggplant. Add rest of the ingredients. Mix well and transfer to the prepared dish. Spread the top evenly with a spatula.

6. Scatter the remaining breadcrumbs on top and sprinkle some paprika.

7. Bake for 30 minutes.

8. Cool for 5 minutes and serve.

Bacon and Goat Cheese Salad

Servings: 3

Ingredients:

- 1 cup chopped endives

- 4 ounces soft goat's cheese, cut into 3 slices

- 1 small egg, beaten

- ½ tablespoon Dijon mustard
- Pepper to taste
- 3 slices bacon
- 1 ½ tablespoons chopped chives
- 1 tablespoon extra-virgin olive oil
- 2 teaspoons red wine vinegar
- 2 slices Atkins cuisine bread
- 2 cups shredded cos or romaine lettuce
- Salt to taste

Directions:

1. Place bacon in a nonstick skillet over medium heat and cook until crisp.
2. Remove with a slotted spoon and place on a plate lined with paper towels. Set aside about a tablespoon of bacon fat and discard the rest.
3. Tear the bread slices and add into the blender. Blend until crumbs are formed. Transfer onto a plate.
4. Place goat cheese slices on the countertop and press

lightly with your hands.

5. Pick one slice of goat cheese and dip in egg. Shake to drop off excess egg.

6. Next, cover cheese slices in breadcrumbs. Press lightly to adhere. Place on a plate.

7. Place a nonstick pan over medium heat. Add half the oil. When the oil is heated, place the goat cheese slices and cook until the underside is golden brown. Flip sides and cook the other side until golden brown.

8. Remove from heat with a slotted spoon and place on a plate lined with paper towels.

9. To make dressing: Add retained bacon fat, remaining oil, mustard, vinegar, and pepper into the hot skillet and stir until well combined.

10. Place bacon and greens in a bowl. Pour the dressing over it and toss well.

11. Divide the salad into 3 plates. Place goat cheese slices on top and serve.

Japanese Vegetable Tofu Soup

Servings: 3

Ingredients:

- 3 cups vegetable broth or chicken broth
- 1 cup chopped bok choy
- ½ tablespoon grated ginger
- ½ serrano pepper, deseeded, minced
- 2 stalks green onions, sliced
- 1 small carrot, shredded
- 2 tablespoons Japanese tamari soy sauce
- 1 cup mixed sliced mushrooms
- 2 cloves garlic, sliced
- ½ cup diced tomatoes
- 3 ounces firm tofu, cut into ½-inch cubes
- 1 tablespoon chopped cilantro to garnish
- Salt to taste
- Pepper to taste

Directions:

1. Pour broth and soy sauce into a saucepan. Place the saucepan over medium heat and bring to a boil.

2. Stir in mushrooms, bok choy, garlic, ginger, and serrano pepper. Lower heat and simmer for 5 minutes.

3. Add remaining ingredients. Heat thoroughly.

4. Ladle into soup bowls. Season with salt and pepper. Garnish with cilantro and serve.

Baked Quesadillas

Servings: 2

Ingredients:

- 1 tablespoon chopped onion
- 4 ounces Monterey Jack cheese
- ½ jalapeño pepper, chopped
- ¼ teaspoon pepper
- 2 low-carb tortillas (maximum 3 grams net carbs per tortilla)
- 1 tablespoon light olive oil

- 8 ounces pork chops or roasts
- 2 tablespoons salsa verde
- 2 tablespoons chopped cilantro

Directions:

1. Preheat oven to 450° Fahrenheit.
2. Place a skillet over medium-high flame. Add ½ tablespoon oil. When the oil is heated, add onion and sauté until translucent.
3. Remove onions with a slotted spoon and place in a bowl.
4. Add ½ teaspoon oil. When the oil is heated, add pork chop. Sprinkle salt and pepper over it. Cook for about 5 minutes. Flip sides and cook the other side for 5 minutes or until cooked to the desired doneness.
5. Remove pork with a slotted spoon and place on your cutting board. When cool enough to handle, chop into bite size chunks. Transfer into the bowl of onion.
6. Add rest of the ingredients except tortillas and oil and mix well.
7. Brush oil on one side of the tortilla. Place on a baking

sheet, with the oiled side facing down.

8. Place half the pork mixture on one half of each tortilla. Fold the other half over the filling.

9. Bake for about 5-8 minutes or until crisp.

Beef and Spinach Soup

Servings: 8

Ingredients:

- 7 ounces shiitake mushrooms
- 4 eggs
- 6 cups chicken broth
- 6 cloves garlic, minced
- 1 lb. ground beef
- 8 ounces oyster mushrooms
- 1 lb. fresh baby spinach
- 2 spring onions, sliced
- 4 tablespoons sesame oil
- 2 tablespoons sesame seeds

- 4 tablespoons soy sauce
- 2 teaspoons salt
- 1 teaspoon pepper

Directions:

1. Place a soup pot over medium heat.
2. Add oil. When the oil is heated, add beef and cook until brown.
3. Add spring onion, garlic, and mushrooms and sauté for a couple of minutes.
4. Add chicken broth and soy sauce and bring to a boil.
5. Add spinach and simmer until spinach wilts. Add salt and pepper.
6. Mix eggs and sesame seeds in a bowl. Pour into the simmering soup, stirring constantly.
7. Simmer for a couple of minutes until bits of egg begin to float on top.
8. Serve in individual soup bowls.

Beef and Vegetable Stew

Servings: 3-4

Ingredients:

- ¾ lb. beef chuck, trimmed of some of the fat
- ½ teaspoon oregano
- ½ teaspoon thyme
- ½ teaspoon rosemary
- 1 teaspoon salt
- 1 tablespoon unsalted butter
- 1 clove garlic, peeled, sliced
- ½ lb. green snap beans
- 1 tablespoon Thick-It-Up (low-carb thickener)
- 1 teaspoon salt
- 1 tablespoon extra-virgin olive oil
- ½ cup white pearl onions
- 8 ounces Merlot wine
- 1 small carrot, chopped

- 1 cup water

Directions:

1. Preheat the oven to 325° Fahrenheit.
2. Place beef in a bowl. Sprinkle salt, pepper, paprika, and herbs and toss well.
3. Place a Dutch oven over medium-high heat. Add oil. When the oil is heated, add beef and cook until brown. Remove beef onto a plate.
4. Add butter to Dutch oven. When butter melts, add onion and sauté until light brown. Add garlic and sauté until aromatic.
5. Add beef and cooked juices back into the pot. Stir in the wine and 1 cup water.
6. When it begins to boil, lower the heat and cover the pot. Transfer the pot into the oven.
7. Bake for about 1 ½ hours or until meat is cooked.
8. Stir in carrots and green beans. When they are cooked, remove the oven and place over medium-high heat on the stovetop.
9. Add Thick-It-Up and mix well. Simmer until thick,

stirring constantly.

10. Taste and adjust the seasoning if required.

11. Ladle into bowls and serve.

Calabacitas

Servings: 3

Ingredients:

- 1 tablespoon canola oil
- ½ fresh jalapeno pepper, chopped
- ¼ cup corn kernels
- ¼ teaspoon chili powder
- 1 small onion, chopped
- 1 lb. zucchini, cut into half-moon slices
- Salt to taste

Directions:

1. Place a skillet over medium heat. Add oil. When oil is heated, add onion and pepper. Sauté until the onion is translucent.

2. Add zucchini, corn, salt, and chili powder and mix well.

3. Cook until zucchini is tender. Add 2 tablespoons water, cover, and cook for a couple of minutes before serving.

Yogurt Berry Cups

Servings: 2

Ingredients:

- 2.6 ounces blueberries
- 7 ounces fresh strawberries, chopped
- ¾ cup Greek yogurt
- 1 teaspoon Splenda (optional)
- 1.5 ounces walnuts, chopped

Directions

1. Add yogurt and Splenda to a bowl and whisk well.

2. Add a tablespoon of yogurt each to 2 dessert bowls.

3. Layer with half the strawberries followed by a tablespoon yogurt followed by blueberries. Next, layer with strawberries and yogurt.

4. Garnish with walnuts, chill, and serve.

Yorkshire Pudding

Servings: 4-5

Ingredients:

- ¼ cup whole grain soy flour
- 3 small eggs
- ½ teaspoon salt or to taste
- ½ teaspoon baking powder
- 1 ounce vital wheat gluten
- ½ cup whole milk
- 3 tablespoons canola oil

Directions:

1. Add soy flour, eggs, gluten, salt, and milk to a bowl and whisk well.

2. Add oil to a baking dish and place the dish in a 350° Fahrenheit preheating oven for 5-8 minutes.

3. Pour the pudding batter into the baking dish and bake for 20 minutes, or until the center is set and light brown.

Pineapple-Coconut Granita

Servings: 2

Ingredients:

- 1 cup chopped, fresh pineapple
- ¼ cup water
- ¼ cup sugar substitute
- ½ teaspoon coconut extract

Directions:

1. Add pineapple to a blender and blend until smooth.
2. Place a small saucepan over high heat. Add water and sugar substitute and stir until dissolved completely. Remove from heat.
3. Add blended pineapple and stir. Add coconut extract and stir.
4. Freeze for 30 minutes in a freezer-safe pan. Remove from the freezer and churn the mixture using a fork. Repeat until completely frozen, then serve in bowls.

Carrot Cake

Servings: 2

Ingredients:

- ½ cup carrot, grated
- 1 large egg
- 2 tablespoons butter, melted
- 1 tablespoon heavy cream
- ¾ cup almond flour
- A handful of crushed walnuts
- 2 teaspoons cinnamon
- 1 teaspoon pumpkin spice
- 1 teaspoon baking powder
- cream cheese frosting to garnish

Directions:

1. Take a bowl, and combine all the dry ingredients, baking powder, pumpkin spice, cinnamon, almond flour, and crushed walnuts, and mix using a spoon.

2. In another bowl, combine all the wet ingredients, egg, melted butter, grated carrot, and heavy cream.

3. Mix wet and dry ingredients together.

4. Place 2 ramekins on a plate and fill them with the above mixture.

5. Microwave them for about 6 minutes or bake for 20 minutes in a 400° Fahrenheit oven.

6. Allow the cake to cool off for about 10 minutes and then turn upside down on a large plate.

7. Decorate with some more crushed walnuts and grated carrot on top and serve immediately.

Chapter 12: Atkins Recipes — Phase 4 (Maintenance)

Apple Oatmeal

Servings: 2

Ingredients:

- ½ cup Greek yogurt
- 2 teaspoons ground cinnamon
- 1 apple, peeled, cored, shredded with large holes of grater
- ¼ cup water
- 2.1 ounces oatmeal
- Splenda to taste

Directions:

1. Place a saucepan over medium-high heat. Add oats and sauté for a couple of minutes, until toasted lightly.
2. Add water and apples and stir.
3. When mixture begins to boil, lower heat, simmer, and

cook for about 10 minutes, or until apples are tender.

4. Add Splenda and cinnamon and cook until thick. Stir frequently.

5. Remove from heat and cool slightly.

6. Serve in bowls with Greek yogurt.

Breakfast Frittata

Servings: 2

Ingredients:

- 2 large eggs
- 2-3 tablespoons cream cheese
- ½ cup sliced mushroom
- ½ cup cooked, chopped bacon
- 2 tablespoons extra virgin olive oil
- ¼ cup sour cream
- 2 ounces cheese, shredded
- 1 cup Steam'ables Harvest Vegetables
- ½ cup water

- ½ teaspoon hot sauce

Directions:

1. Place a nonstick pan over medium heat. Add oil. When oil is heated, add mushrooms and vegetables and sauté until mushrooms are tender.

2. Add eggs, sour cream, hot sauce, and water to a bowl and whisk well. Pour into the pan. Do not stir.

3. Sprinkle cheese, bacon, and cream cheese on top.

4. Cover and cook for 3-4 minutes or until set. For frittata, cut into wedges and serve. For omelet, flip and cook the other side before serving.

Egg-Filled Bell Pepper Rings with Fruit

Servings: 2

Ingredients:

- ½ cup shredded, full-fat mozzarella cheese
- ½ small banana, chopped
- 1 kiwi, peeled, chopped
- ½ cup raspberries

- ½ small apple, chopped

- 2 teaspoons extra virgin olive oil

- 4 large eggs

- 1 large sweet red pepper, cut into 4 1-inch thick rings

Directions:

1. Place a skillet over medium-high heat. Add oil. When the oil is heated, place the bell pepper rings in the skillet.

2. Crack an egg into each bell pepper ring.

3. Sprinkle a little water around the bell peppers and cook until the eggs are cooked to the desired doneness.

4. Sprinkle mozzarella cheese on top and transfer to a plate.

5. Mix fruit in a bowl and serve alongside the bell pepper rings.

Strawberry Mousse

Servings: 8

Ingredients:

- 2 packages (4 servings each) instant sugar-free vanilla pudding mix

- 1 ⅓ cups nonfat dry milk powder

- 1 teaspoon vanilla extract

- 2 packages (4 servings each) sugar-free strawberry gelatin mix

- 2 ⅔ cups fresh strawberries, sliced

- 2 tablespoons light whipped cream

Directions:

1. Add the pudding mix, gelatin mix, and milk powder to a large bowl.

2. Place strawberries in another bowl and mash with a little water. Add this to the bowl of pudding mix. Whisk well.

3. Add vanilla extract and cream. Whisk well.

4. Divide into dessert bowls. Cover with cling wrap. Refrigerate for a minimum of 30 minutes before serving.

Conclusion

I want to thank you for choosing this book.

People across the world are worried about gaining weight, and they are doing whatever they can to lose some of their unwanted weight. The Atkins diet is one of the best low-carb diets created, and this book sheds some light on it. This diet has certainly revolutionized the world of fitness with its innovative observations. By making a couple of simple changes to your diet, you can attain your weight loss and fitness goals.

The Atkins diet is so much more than a diet in a conventional sense. It is a way of life which will help improve your overall health by working well with your body metabolism. A diet which improves your metabolism is the best way to lose weight. Unlike other fad diets, this diet is sustainable in the long run. There are various benefits this diet provides, and they aren't restricted to weight loss. The Atkins diet is one of the best low-carb diets created, and this book has shed some light on it.

In this book, you were given all the information that you will need to get started with the Atkins diet. This book will essentially act as your guide as you get started with the Atkins diet. In this book, you were given information about the basics of the Atkins diet, the four phases of this diet, the benefits it offers, and certain facts to replace the popular myths about this diet. You were also given simple steps and tips which will help you get started with this diet and stay on course. Apart from this, you now have information about the different macros and the breakdown of macros in the different phases of this diet.

Getting started with a new diet is a major lifestyle change and you will need all the help you can get to make this transition. By using the different recipes provided in this book, you can start cooking delicious and nutritious meals in no time. While you shop for groceries, ensure that you follow the Atkins food list in this book. By stocking your pantry with Atkins-friendly foods, it certainly becomes easier to stick to the diet.

By keeping track of your macros, you will be able to find the foods that work well for your metabolism. When you eat foods that help your metabolism, it will not only improve your overall health, but it will also help you lose weight. If you want to do this, then you need to have a plan of action. By following the steps given in this book, you can ease your way into the Atkins diet. This book will help you do all this in no time.

Now, all you need to do is get started as soon as you can! Remember that the key to a healthier life lies in your hands.

Patience, conscious effort, and consistency will help you attain your weight loss and fitness goals!

Thank you and good luck!

References

Atkins. (n.d.). Phase 1 - Frequently Asked Questions. Retrieved from https://sa.atkins.com/why-atkins/the-phases/phase-1-induction/phase-1-frequently-asked-questions.html

Atkins. (n.d.). 8 Tips on How to Start the Atkins Diet. Retrieved from https://www.atkins.com/how-it-works/library/articles/how-to-start-the-atkins-diet-tips-for-beginners

Atkins. (n.d.). Phase 1 – Induction. Retrieved from https://sa.atkins.com/why-atkins/the-phases/phase-1-induction/

Atkins. (n.d.). Phase 2 - Frequently Asked Questions. Retrieved from https://au.atkins.com/why-atkins/the-phases/phase-2-ongoing-weight-loss/phase-2-frequently-asked-questions.html

Atkins. (n.d.). Phase 3 - Frequently Asked Questions. Retrieved from https://au.atkins.com/why-atkins/the-phases/phase-3-pre-maintenance/phase-3-frequently-asked-questions.html

Atkins. (n.d.). Phase 4 - Frequently Asked Questions.

Retrieved from https://au.atkins.com/why-atkins/the-phases/phase-4-maintenance/phase-4-frequently-asked-questions.html

Atkins. (n.d.). The Phases. Retrieved from https://sa.atkins.com/why-atkins/the-phases/

Doc's Opinion. (2012). The Atkins Diet. Retrieved from https://www.docsopinion.com/health-and-nutrition/diets/the-atkins-diet/

Dolson, L. (2019). What to Expect on the Atkins Diet. Retrieved from https://www.verywellfit.com/atkins-diet-what-to-expect-2241655#modifications

Gunnars, K. (2018, August 2). The Atkins Diet: Everything You Need to Know. Retrieved from https://www.healthline.com/nutrition/atkins-diet-101#foods-to-avoid

Klein, A. (2008, August 22). Atkins Diet: What You Need to Know. Retrieved from https://health.howstuffworks.com/wellness/diet-fitness/diets/atkins2.htm

Mayo Clinic. (2017, August 29). Can a low-carb diet help you lose weight? Retrieved from https://www.mayoclinic.org/healthy-lifestyle/weight-loss/in-

depth/
low-carb-diet/art-20045831?pg=2

Mayo Clinic. (2017, August 16). Atkins Diet: What's behind the claims? Retrieved from https://www.mayoclinic.org/healthy-lifestyle/weight-loss/in-depth/atkins-diet/art-20048485?pg=2

Miller, J. (2017, April 04). 15 Health Benefits of the Atkins Diet, According to Science (How to Get Started/Diet Plan). Retrieved from https://www.jenreviews.com/atkins-diet/#What_are_the_health_benefits_of_the_Atkins_diet

NHS UK. (2018). The Truth About Carbs. Retrieved from https://www.nhs.uk/live-well/healthy-weight/why-we-need-to-eat-carbs/

Nordqvist, C. (2017, April 13). Atkins diet: Phases, Atkins 40, foods to eat and avoid. Retrieved from https://www.medicalnewstoday.com/articles/7379.php

WebMD. (n.d.). Atkins Diet: Phases, Meal Plans, and Weight Loss. Retrieved from https://www.webmd.com/diet/atkins-diet-what-you-can-eat#1-3

White, M. (2013, February 20). Atkins Diet Vitamins and Supplements - based on Dr Atkins own advice. Retrieved from https://low-carb-support.com/vitamins-supplements-for-atkins-diet/

Made in the
USA
Middletown, DE